D1710410

Gregory Hines

ENTERTAINER

Black Americans of Achievement

LEGACY EDITION

Muhammad Ali
Maya Angelou
Josephine Baker
George Washington Carver
Johnnie Cochran
Frederick Douglass
W.E.B. Du Bois
Marcus Garvey
Savion Glover
Alex Haley
Jimi Hendrix
Gregory Hines
Langston Hughes
Jesse Jackson
Scott Joplin
Coretta Scott King
Martin Luther King, Jr.
Malcolm X
Bob Marley
Thurgood Marshall
Barack Obama
Jesse Owens
Rosa Parks
Colin Powell
Condoleezza Rice
Chris Rock
Sojourner Truth
Harriet Tubman
Nat Turner
Booker T. Washington
Oprah Winfrey
Tiger Woods

Gregory Hines

ENTERTAINER

Dennis Abrams

CHELSEA HOUSE
PUBLISHERS
An imprint of Infobase Publishing

Gregory Hines

Chelsea House
An imprint of Infobase Publishing
132 West 31st Street
New York NY 10001

Library of Congress Cataloging-in-Publication Data

Abrams, Dennis, 1960-
  Gregory Hines / Dennis Abrams.
     p. cm. -- (Black Americans of achievement)
  Includes bibliographical references and index.
  ISBN 978-0-7910-9718-2 (hardcover : alk. paper) 1. Hines, Gregory--Juvenile literature.
2. Actors--United States--Biography--Juvenile literature. 3. African American actors--
Biography--Juvenile literature. I. Title. II. Series.
  PN2287.H53D46 2008
  791.43'028'092--dc22
  [B]   2007045506

Chelsea House books are available at special discounts when purchased in bulk quantities for businesses, associations, institutions, or sales promotions. Please call our Special Sales Department in New York at (212) 967-8800 or (800) 322-8755.

You can find Chelsea House on the World Wide Web at
http://www.chelseahouse.com

Series design by Keith Trego
Cover design by Keith Trego and Jooyoung An

Printed in the United States of America

Bang ML 10 9 8 7 6 5 4 3 2 1

This book is printed on acid-free paper.

Contents

"I Am a Tap Dancer"

The death of a beloved entertainer always comes as a shock to the general public. Fans look forward to watching the performer entertain them and begin to feel that he or she will always be around. They feel comfortable in the performer's presence, and they may even think of the performer as a member of the family. When the performer dies young, it comes as an even greater shock: the loss of their presence is combined with the loss of future artistry. Such a performer was tap dancer extraordinaire Gregory Hines, who died of cancer of the liver on August 9, 2003. He was only 57 years old.

His loss was felt throughout the United States and, indeed, around the world. Broadway theater fans looked back fondly at his performances in such hits as *Eubie!*, *Sophisticated Ladies*, and especially *Jelly's Last Jam*, for which he won the theater's top prize, the Tony Award. Film fans recalled his memorable roles in *History of the World, Part I*, *The Cotton*

Gregory Hines and Bernadette Peters cohost the 2002 Tony Awards at Radio City Music Hall in New York City. Founded in 1947, the Tony Awards recognize excellence in Broadway productions and performances. Hines was nominated for five Tony Awards and won for Best Actor in a Musical for his performance in *Jelly's Last Jam.*

Club, White Nights, Running Scared, and *Tap.* Television audiences remembered his winning performances in his own short-lived series *The Gregory Hines Show* and his roles on *Will and Grace* and *Lost at Home.* As a result of his diverse body of work, Gregory Hines touched the lives of many people.

Hines moved audiences and fellow performers alike; they all realized what had been lost with his passing. Broadway legend Bernadette Peters, who had appeared with Hines as cohost of the 2002 Tony Awards said, "His dancing came from something very real. It came out of his instincts, his impulses and his amazing creativity. His whole heart and soul went into everything he did."

George C. Wolfe, who directed Hines in *Jelly's Last Jam,* said that Hines "was the last of a kind of immaculate performer—a singer, dancer, actor and a personality. He knew how to command."

Even though Hines earned widespread acclaim as a singer and actor, he is best remembered as a tap dancer. A dancer since he was just a toddler and a performer since he was five, Hines had honed and expanded his craft until he changed the concept of what was possible in tap. He was widely acknowledged as the greatest tap dancer of his generation.

In an article in the *New York Times* entitled "An Appreciation; Gregory Hines: From Time Step to Timeless," author Sally R. Sommer illustrated Hines's style, explained how it grew from the past, and showed its influence on all tap dancers to come:

> The older tap masters Hines admired . . . possessed old-school elegance and polished skills. They dressed sharply and danced in an easy, swinging upright style. No matter how funny—how "down"—they might get, they were always pre-1950s gentlemen. And they always kept good time.
>
> Then Hines broke the codes. By his national dance tour in 1986, he had perfected the new image. Suddenly the tapper was sexy, muscled, new-school and macho. Hines worked out at the gym so the T-shirt was tight, the body had substance, and the line was strong. Hunkered over like a prizefighter, unsmiling, he cocked his head and stared at the floor as if looking for answers.

Gregory Hines gestures during a rehearsal for *Jelly's Last Jam*. An article in the *New York Times* credited Hines with changing the concept of a tap dancer; whereas old-school masters "possessed...elegance and polished skills," Hines was "sexy, muscled, new-school and macho."

Hines danced hard and messy, sometimes slurring his sounds angrily. He threw in African dance moves that revealed deeper, older connections. He designed a miked portable stage to amplify the taps and put the tap-dancer on equal footing with the loud music. He played his floor like a drum, testing the surface until he found "the spot," sounding the wood for melodies, pitches and thunks.

Certainly, he had a hip, cool presence. But with Hines the cool always slipped . . . when Hines danced hard, a gap of skin always showed between the bottom of his pants and the top of his socks. His shoelaces seemed too long. Or in the middle of a phrase, he would suddenly stop, wipe his brow, take a swig from a water bottle and start chatting to the audience.

According to Sommer, perhaps the biggest break Hines made from tap dancers of the past was in his rhythms. Escaping the basic four-square tempos of traditional tap, he seemed to move to his own rhythms, changing pace at whim and bringing tap into the world of modern dance. Sommer concluded by saying, "Hines's break with the sacred tap traditions was monumental. It jerked tap out of a pre-1950s aesthetic and pushed it into the 1990s and beyond. He renewed tap by roughing it up and giving it emotional weight."

It is important to note that artists, regardless of whether they are dancers, writers, painters, or anything else, cannot change their chosen art form overnight. It takes years of sweat, work, and practice to learn the basics, the traditions of one's art, before they can then go ahead and forge their own style.

Gregory Hines was no exception to this rule. Indeed, although he had tapped nearly as long as he had walked, he was in his late thirties before he felt comfortable enough with his dancing that he found his true style. It was then that he began to "relax and reach true expression," as he said in the television special *Gregory Hines: Tap Dance in America*.

Indeed, it had been quite a journey to get to that stage. Hines began his career as a child performer, working with his brother and then later with his brother and father in nightclubs,

DID YOU KNOW?

Did you know that, due to the resurgent popularity of tap dancing, May 25 is now National Tap Dance Day? The bill was signed into law in 1989. May 25 was chosen because it is the birthday of famous tapper Bill "Bojangles" Robinson.

theaters, and television before leaving the act in 1973. Anxious to start a new life, he left his family and friends behind in New York City and fled to Venice, California, where he gave up on tap, started a rock band, and lived a life of, as he put it, "music, women and drugs," before returning to New York with a new attitude and confidence that quickly made him a Broadway star. Once established on Broadway, he moved on to conquer the worlds of movies and television.

He wasn't exactly an overnight sensation. How did he do it? What attracted Gregory Hines to tap? How did he go from being a dance dropout to becoming the preeminent tap dancer of his generation as well as a TV and movie star? A legendary tap dancer from an earlier generation, John Sublett (known as John Bubbles), once said, "Listen to my feet, and I will tell you the story of my life." The same is true for Gregory Hines.

Tapping to Success

Gregory Oliver Hines was born on February 14, 1946, in New York City. He was the second son of Alma Iola and Maurice Hines. The family lived in Washington Heights, an ethnically mixed neighborhood near the northern tip of Manhattan's Upper West Side. The neighborhood is just north of Harlem, which was the home of some of the most famous African-American entertainers, including singer Ethel Waters and jazz great Louis Armstrong. Several well-known tap dancers also lived there, among them the Nicholas Brothers, famous for combining traditional tap dancing with ballet and energetic acrobatics, and Bill "Bojangles" Robinson, known for his innovative and seemingly effortless tapping.

Alma and Maurice Hines decided it would be a good idea for Gregory's older brother, Maurice Jr., to learn tap dancing, and they signed him up for lessons. (As Gregory pointed out in a later interview, "My parents gave my brother, Maurice, and

I tap lessons, I think, like parents give their children piano or saxophone, just something to round them out.") Maurice Jr. was just over four years old.

Hines's mother recalled the first day Maurice Jr. went for tap lessons. Gregory was two and a half—too young to take lessons—but he cried until the teacher let him in. Alma Hines said, "I looked in the door, and Greg was holding on to his brother's hand doing the tap, and with his other hand he had his thumb in his mouth." Little Gregory was still too young to actually take lessons, but he copied a lot of tap steps from his brother.

Apparently the boys had a natural talent for the art, as well as an eagerness to learn. Others in the family had aspired to be performers, as well. Their paternal grandmother, Ora Hines, had been a showgirl at Harlem's famed Cotton Club during the 1920s. Their father, although he was working as a grocery clerk when Gregory was born, had musical ambitions. There was another consideration, as Gregory later recalled: "There was the feeling maybe this could be a way of earning a living."

Maurice Hines Sr., who had changed jobs to become a bouncer at the Audubon Theater and Ballroom in Harlem, sometimes got the boys onto the stage during fashion shows. Their performances were short, but they did earn a little money. The brothers' careers in show business had just begun, although the boys' skills were still minimal.

IN HIS OWN WORDS...

From the introduction to *Brotherhood in Rhythm*: "The Nicholas Brothers were in a league of their own. They glittered. They flashed. 'Uncorked genies,' as the critic Arlene Croce described them, the brothers flew through acrobatic feats so astounding that projectionists sometimes had to rewind films and replay their dance routines for clamoring audiences."

Henry LeTang became a tap legend for his teaching and choreography. LeTang taught Maurice and Gregory Hines when they were children and remained in their lives as a guiding presence. Above, Gregory Hines and LeTang pose at the 2002 American Choreography Awards, where LeTang was honored.

After the boys took group classes at the local tap school and showed some ability, their parents were able to get them lessons with one of the best tap dance teachers available—Henry LeTang. LeTang had taken his first tap dance lessons at the age of 7 and opened his first dance studio at 17, going on to instruct some of America's greatest entertainers.

He was just the instructor the Hines brothers needed. As Maurice said in a 2006 interview, "Henry LeTang was a great teacher for Gregory and me. Henry gave us the love of the dance." Gregory added, "He gave us an act. That was really the beginning." After lessons with Henry LeTang, the Hines boys began performing professionally. Maurice Jr. was eight years old, and Gregory was six.

In an interview with National Public Radio (NPR) in 1989, Hines discussed the process that led to him performing professionally at such an early age:

> I think it was just a group decision, Henry, my parents, and I suppose, some of the members of the family. In those days, tap dancing was still very highly respected and an area that a lot of people wanted to be in. And the Nicholas Brothers were big stars at that time, and it was Henry's contention that we would be the second coming of the Nicholas Brothers. . . . I mean, there was work, and you know, we were cute, and we could dance, and we enjoyed it.

Billing themselves as the Hines Kids, Maurice Jr. and Gregory began appearing at Harlem's famed Apollo Theater. The Apollo Theater, which for many years was the only theater in New York to hire black talent, billed itself as a place "where stars are born and legends are made." It became famous for launching the careers of such legendary stars as Ella Fitzgerald, Billie Holiday, James Brown, The Jackson 5, and Lauryn Hill.

The theater served as a kind of day-care center for the boys. Their mother took them there after school and then picked them up at night after their last show. At the Apollo, the boys had the opportunity to watch many famous performers, including Sammy Davis Jr., whom Gregory wanted to emulate.

In 1955, at the suggestion of Alma Hines, the boys began making the rounds of the nightclubs, performing only on

weekends during the school year and then touring more exten-
sively during summer vacations. Around this time, Gregory
had an accident that affected his vision for the rest of his life.
While playing one day, he fell on a tree stump, an accident
that left him legally blind in his right eye. That mishap did not
interrupt his busy dancing schedule for long, however.

Although their schedule kept them busy working, they weren't
making a lot of money. As Hines said in his NPR interview,

> Well, we made money, but not much. I mean, in those
> days, you know, there really wasn't much money, and it was
> beginning to diminish as we were performing, because tap
> dancing was beginning to go out, so there really wasn't a
> lot of money. I think some of those early jobs, maybe we
> made $25 for, you know, what was known as a club date.
> I remember New Year's Eve was a big night, and that per-
> formers would get paid double. So maybe New Year's Eve,
> we'd get paid $50 for a club date, but there really wasn't a
> lot of money.

Besides performing in nightclubs, Maurice Jr. and Gregory
appeared on television's *The Jackie Gleason Show* and even did
some stints in Europe. As the boys grew older, they changed
the name of their act. When "we started to get pimples,"
Gregory later commented, they began calling themselves the
Hines Brothers.

The boys even appeared on *The Ed Sullivan Show*, which
was the premier television variety show for entertainers of
all kinds. As an adult, Gregory had very few memories of the
appearance, but he did remember one thing that happened
after the brothers danced. In those days, black male entertainers often wore a lot of grease in their hair, which slicked it
down and gave them "respect." After the brothers danced, Sullivan came over to them to thank them, they took a bow, and

Sullivan put his hand on Gregory's head. You can only imagine how shocked he was when he realized that "he had at least an ounce of grease on his hands!"

The years on the road must have been hard on the family. Alma Hines traveled with the boys, and Maurice Sr. stayed at home. The separations did have a bright side, however. While Maurice Sr. was on his own, he learned to play the drums. That way, he was able to join the act so that the family could stay

Sammy Davis Jr.

Sammy Davis Jr. (1925–1990) was one of the great American entertainers. He was a dancer, singer, multi-instrumentalist (he could play vibraphone, trumpet, and drums), impressionist, comedian, and Broadway, movie, and television actor. It seemed that there was nothing he could not do.

Born in Harlem to two entertainers, Davis joined the act with his father and adopted uncle Will Mastin as a young child. Mastin and his father did their best to shield him from racism, but as he grew up, he became aware of the attitudes many people had about him simply because he was black.

After he achieved superstar status, Davis refused to work at venues that practiced segregation. His demands eventually led to the integration of Miami Beach nightclubs and casinos in Las Vegas, Nevada. He was particularly proud of this accomplishment. During his early years in Vegas, Davis and other African American artists could entertain on the stage, but they frequently could not stay at the very hotels at which they performed, and they definitely could not gamble in the casinos, use the pool, or go to the hotel restaurants and bars.

Davis was one of the hardest working people in show business. For example, in 1964, he starred in the Broadway musical *Golden Boy* at night, shot his own New York-based afternoon talk show during the day, and when he could get a day off from the theater, he would either be in the studio recording new songs or performing live, often at charity benefits as far away as Miami, Chicago, and Las Vegas, or doing television variety specials in Los Angeles. He once said that he was incapable of standing still. All that hard work paid off: Davis is remembered and loved as one of the greatest all-around entertainers who ever lived. Without him, and his simple demand for racial equality, careers such as Gregory Hines's would not have been the same.

Maurice Hines Sr. learned to play the drums while his sons were on the road with their traveling act. In 1963, he joined the act, which was renamed "Hines, Hines and Dad." This enabled the family to stay together and continue working. The three Hines men are shown above in a photograph from 1971.

together while touring. In 1963, when Gregory's father came on board, the act was renamed Hines, Hines and Dad—with Maurice Jr. playing the "straight man" to Gregory's "comic relief."

Young Gregory was happy that his father had joined the act, but his father was even happier because the family could spend more time together. In those days, before television programs like *The Cosby Show,* there were very few positive images in the media of a black family that stayed together, worked together, and enjoyed each other's company. By performing as a family, he believed that he could bring a positive image of blacks to the public, both black and white.

The trio toured for several years, playing Las Vegas and making television appearances on *The Tonight Show Starring Johnny Carson.* Gregory insisted, however, that "we weren't ever really successful. . . . We were a very strong opening act, but we never got over the hump."

How did Gregory Hines feel about working as a professional during his childhood? Did he think his parents pushed him too hard? Not too hard, Hines said in 1985. His parents signed their sons up for lessons "like parents give kids violin lessons, and when we showed a little aptitude they just decided to see if it was something we could use. . . . Our mother wanted us to have an outlet," said Gregory. His brother Maurice added, "to get us out of the ghetto." Gregory explained that their mother was particularly supportive of her sons' talents but did not push them unwillingly into the business. Did he feel, as many young performers do later on, that he missed out on having a carefree childhood? "It was fun," he said in a 1996 interview. "It didn't feel like a job, even though we were on the road appearing in nightclubs all over the country. We had a childhood too, so it was great." He later told another interviewer:

> My mother was able to make it enjoyable. My brother and I would come offstage at the Apollo—we were doing four shows a day. She would take off our clothes, rub us down with alcohol [a massage, similar to the kind given to athletes after a tough game], put our bathrobes on and comic books in our hands, and feed us from the two-eye burner she had in the dressing room.

Hines spent most of his childhood in Washington Heights. He often claimed, however, that he grew up in the neighboring Harlem area. "I don't know where he gets this Harlem bit," said his mother in 1986. Certainly Gregory spent a great deal of time and energy at the Apollo Theater, where he learned so much from his mentors and other performers. Perhaps he felt, as an African American, that he could more strongly identify with the neighborhood of Harlem than with the one he lived in.

Hines, like many African Americans, did have white ancestry on his mother's side. Her ancestors were Jewish, Panamanian, Irish, and Portuguese—not solely African American. Hines explained his feelings about his own racial identity: "I have always considered myself a black man. What my mother has on her side is irrelevant. When I go for a role that was written for a white, it means nothing."

One more personal factor contributed to Gregory's feelings about race and his place as a black man. He said in an interview with *Cigar Aficionado* magazine that "I come from a background where people on my mother's side of the family are very light-skinned and the people on my father's side are dark-skinned. And when my mother married my father, my mother's father refused to come to the wedding. He didn't want her to marry a dark-skinned African American."

Perhaps because of this, Hines took a special pride in being black. He spoke fondly of childhood memories that introduced him to what he called "race pride": for example, picking up a magazine and seeing a black face on the cover or watching Jackie Robinson play baseball.

In many ways, though, Gregory and Maurice Jr. were protected from the racism that was still common throughout the country. The young Hines brothers attended Willard Mace, a special school for professional children. At the time, they were the only black students. Later, the boys attended the Quintano School for Young Professionals, where other future performers such as Patty Duke, Sal Mineo, and Bernadette Peters also studied. Because Gregory and his brother went to school with fellow performers, they did not stand out; in their world, that was normal. In that world, the brothers' race was also largely irrelevant. Perhaps as a result, Hines claimed that he always felt at ease around white people and felt accepted because of his talent and charm.

Nevertheless, racism was still a prevalent attitude throughout the United States. From years of traveling and performing, the Hines brothers had learned about the world of entertainment and dance. Within that world, although they were black, they were accepted because of their talent. There was another world, however, outside the stage, and Gregory and Maurice Jr. were soon exposed to it as well. Hines later put it in simple terms: "Miami. Nineteen-fifty-seven. That's where I really discovered what was happening."

Segregation was still the law of the land, particularly in the Deep South. African Americans were forced to live apart from whites; they could not travel in white areas without police passes. In 1957, 11-year-old Gregory and the cast of his revue were picking up their passes in a police station in Miami Beach. Being thirsty, young Gregory headed for a water fountain—the white one. The fountain for blacks was labeled "Colored," so young Gregory thought the water might be some sort of color. "I got within a few feet, and about twenty of the black people in the show came running over and grabbed me," he recalled. "And I figured the whole thing out." Later, Hines remarked of the incident that "those were the conditions. You lived within those conditions and pushed to change, but you knew the score."

Hines was aware of and angered and saddened by the racism that was still alive in America. He gained new assurance and confidence through the accomplishments of the great African-American sprinter Wilma Rudolph at the 1960 Olympics. As he told NPR,

She was something special to me. I was 14, and it was racism like crazy. It was subtle, because I was living in New York; but I felt it. Hearing all this stuff about white folks being better than us and wondering "Do we measure up?" They were saying we didn't, and just being aware of the supposed differences made me uncomfortable. And then there was Wilma Rudolph. Just watching the way she ran—so beautiful, so graceful and she made it all look so effortless. When she won one, then another and another gold medal, I knew it wasn't true, all the things they said.

On the whole though, Hines felt that his "was a wonderful childhood." He spent most of his time learning more about the history of tap dancing as well as the techniques, and he realized that he had the rare opportunity to meet and interact with his idols. "I grew up surrounded by great black tap dancers," Hines said in a 1986 interview. His tap teacher, the legendary Henry LeTang, told him and his brother that "you two better learn to really dance, because now you're cute, but cute's not for long."

Gregory Hines took his teacher's words to heart, eventually becoming one of the foremost interpreters of modern tap. It would not be easy, though. To go beyond being a cute "novelty act" and to become a real dancer, he would have to absorb the history of tap and then move beyond it. Hines had a lot to learn before he could take part in the evolution of tap.

3

Developing a Style

Gregory Hines had his own ideas about the evolution and history of tap dancing. When asked if tap is a black tradition, he responded:

> I don't know. There's always been an argument as to who invented tap dancing. I went out to dinner with [American dancer, singer, director, and choreographer] Gene Kelly once . . . he felt that it had come from the Irish clog dances. I have always felt that African-American tap dancers took tap dancing and tried to express themselves in a spontaneous and improvisational way. And because our experience is so intertwined with jazz music, which is an American art form, there was a fusion between tap dancers and jazz musicians that kicked tap dancing to another level in terms of growth. So, as an African-American tap dancer, I'm very proud of our contribution.

Gene Kelly (right), an actor, dancer, and director, dances with Frank Sinatra in a scene from *Take Me Out to the Ballgame*. Kelly was a major exponent of filmed dance. According to Gregory Hines, Kelly thought American tap dancing had its roots in Irish clog dancing.

If Gene Kelly believed that tap dancing has its roots in Irish dancing, and Hines believed that African Americans created jazz tap, it seems likely that both were correct. Like any American art form, it appears that tap is a mixture of many influences, created by many people of different ethnic origins. Noted tap historian Rusty Frank, author of the book *TAP! The Greatest Tap Dance Stars and Their Stories 1900–1955,* described tap as the meshing of many different dance styles brought to the United States by people of predominantly African, English, Irish, and Scottish origin. Those styles then mingled with ragtime, jazz, swing, and bebop to evolve into modern tap. Frank also believed that tap took its spirit from the rhythms and tempo of the Machine Age in the United States, taking its sound from what he called the "clickety-clack of electric streetcars, the crash and pound of the subway, the riveting cry of buildings going up and coming down."

Tap's origins in the 1800s show that improvisation and competition were key elements in its development. Jane Goldberg, a tap historian, wrote that tap "came out of the lower classes, developed in competitive 'battles' on street corners by Irish immigrants and African-American slaves." (These "battles" are similar to today's "rap battles," such as the one seen in the Eminem movie *8 Mile*.) From tap's earliest roots in the 1800s, "challenges" and "stealing steps" were common. One-upmanship was a hallmark of tap, and stealing steps did not mean just imitating others. A dancer always added his or her own spin to the steps. As early as the 1840s, tap originator William Henry "Juba" Lane and Irish step dancer Jack Diamond challenged each other in dance competitions in Boston and New York City. Neither was a clear winner.

African Americans and Irish immigrants had certain things in common in the nineteenth century. As slaves, African Americans were forbidden to play drums, an essential part of most African music and dance. Instead, they developed a form of dance involving hand clapping and foot tapping. In Ireland, the British rulers of the island had outlawed Irish cultural activities such as traditional Irish music and dancing. In the United States, too, immigrants from both groups were mostly poor, and the majority of white society looked upon them as outcasts. Over time, Irish clog dancing and African-American dance and syncopation melded together. With additions contributed along the way by a variety of artists, the art form we know today as tap came into being.

Whatever its deepest roots, tap is a distinctly modern (and American) form of dance. Tap reached its peak popularity in the first decades of the twentieth century. Particularly after World War I, during the Roaring Twenties, jazz grew in popularity, and jazz dance (what we know as tap dancing) took the youth culture of the day by storm. (Rock and roll music had much the same effect on the country's youth in the 1950s.)

This new style of dance had spread from the black minstrel shows of the late nineteenth century to the vaudeville shows of the early twentieth century on to the concert stage and later to Broadway musicals. These were also the years when Hollywood films made the transition from silent to sound. With the birth of sound movies came the musical, a form that relies heavily on singing and dancing. Hollywood gave Americans what they wanted to see, thus providing tap dancing with an essential place in the new musical films.

In turn, films also helped to spread tap's popularity; people wanted to see live what they saw in movies. Wherever audiences wanted entertainment, tap artists—"hoofers" as they were called—were sure to be there, dancing their way through small towns and large cities.

Although the "golden age" of tap dancing in Hollywood musicals was the 1930s through the 1950s, the Hines family was still able to make a living touring and tapping into the 1970s. Gregory and Maurice Jr. were born at a time when tap was still a hot form of entertainment and, therefore, a viable profession. Tap, as a form of expression, is still evolving today, but it was the great dancers in tap's golden age who raised tap dancing to an art form.

Who were some of those dancers who helped develop tap into what it is today? Who were Hines's mentors? Who influenced him the most?

INFLUENCES

In an interview in 1992, Hines was asked what he had "picked up" from Sammy Davis Jr., a noted black entertainer (1925–1990). Hines replied:

I met Sammy Davis Jr. when I was about nine years old, and it seemed that every time I was in his company, I learned from him. He was extremely generous with his knowledge and experiences. I idolized him. . . . He knew that I idolized him, but he was never in any way aloof with me; he was never intimidating. I always felt that he was a real person, and in many ways, that's shaped me. Because in this business, where someone is in front of the public a lot and blown up and praised, some people begin to feel distanced. They begin to think that that person is not human. Sammy Davis was so sincere and honest with me; it touched me in a way that shaped me as a person and as an artist.

Other dancers Hines included among his heroes were Harold and Fayard Nicholas (known professionally as the Nicholas Brothers), Jimmy Slyde, and Bunny Briggs. Each of these artists influenced tap with his own individual style. The Nicholas Brothers were known as "The Show Stoppers" at the legendary Cotton Club in Harlem and appeared in several films during the 1930s and 1940s. One of these, 1943's *Stormy Weather*, features a nearly unbelievable dance sequence in which the brothers' fast-paced dancing is punctuated with leaps and splits. Jimmy Slyde incorporated elaborate slides in his dancing; these soon became his trademark. Bunny Briggs, too, was unique in his elegant, gentle style of tapping that accompanied many of the most famous big bands, such as Duke Ellington and his orchestra.

Did any of these dancers directly influence the Hines Brothers' style? Certainly the Nicholas Brothers did, as Gregory described in his NPR interview:

It was Henry's [their tap instructor, Henry LeTang] contention that we would be the second coming of the Nicholas Brothers. And, in fact, my brother and I patterned ourselves after them. I latched onto Harold, and my brother used his

Sammy Davis Jr. dances during a rehearsal at the Victoria Palace in London in 1960. Davis and Gregory Hines first met when Hines was nine years old and worked together later in their lives, most notably in the movie *Tap*.

hands and danced like Fayard, so we just started working . . . but in no way did we compare to the Nicholas Brothers in terms of the kind of acrobatic things that they were doing. We did some flips and some knee drops we called them in those days. That's where one leg is straight and the other leg is slightly bent. Nicholas Brothers used to do complete splits, but our style wasn't into the acrobatics. We were more tap, mostly tap and a lot of syncopated combinations.

One might wonder if being surrounded by older, more experienced dancers and entertainers was intimidating for the younger Hines brother. How did the boys manage to get along with each other and still develop their own individual styles? Gregory explained the differences: "My style of tap is more improvisational. . . . My brother had much more of a choreographic aspect, working things out beforehand." He also explained that a hallmark of great tap dancing is individuality, recalling: "Well, one of the things about tap dancers, they just have so many different styles. Bill Robinson was up on his toes. John Bubbles, of Buck and Bubbles . . . was down on his heels. So you learned very early on to respect everybody's style."

Both brothers were greatly influenced by the stars of the 1950s, whom they saw and interacted with at the Apollo Theater. The young Gregory marveled at the discipline of the performers he saw there. As he recalled later,

> One day, at the first show, I see this guy Teddy Hale, and I think, "Wow, he's tremendous!" Comes out for the second show—and does a completely different dance! I can't figure it out! By the third show, I figure out that he doesn't have an act—he just makes it up as he goes along. I had no barometer to measure this guy. And from that point on, I decided that I wanted to be Teddy Hale.

When Hines performed over school vacations, his backstage time was well spent. He made it a point to approach dancers and ask them to draw him some steps. Then he went off by himself and made up his own routines based on what he had learned.

Hines also had the more usual experience of watching his idols on television. "I've stolen lots of steps from greats like Fred Astaire, Gene Kelly, and the Nicholas Brothers. I watched them on TV and learned from them," he admitted to an interviewer. So what was Gregory Hines's signature style? What was it that made his dancing unmistakably his? He was known for dancing what he terms "improvography"—a word he coined. He preferred to do "riffs," like a jazz musician does with a well-known melody. He took liberties with rhythms, making up his steps as he went along. Such improvisation is considered the highest form of creation, demanding that a tapper's imagination translate immediately into instant choreography.

Fred Astaire

Fred Astaire (May 10, 1899–June 22, 1987), born Frederick Austerlitz in Omaha, Nebraska, was an American film and Broadway stage dancer, choreographer, singer, and actor. His stage and subsequent film career spanned a total of 76 years, and during that time, he made 31 musical films. He is particularly associated with Ginger Rogers, with whom he costarred in 10 films that revolutionized the movie musical.

Although Astaire called himself a simple entertainer, legendary ballet choreographer George Balanchine and famous ballet dancer Rudolf Nureyev both rated him as the greatest dancer of the twentieth century. Generally acknowledged as the most influential dancer in the history of filmed and televised musicals, he was named the fifth greatest male film star legend in the first century of American film by the American Film Institute (AFI).

The AFI honor is somewhat ironic, because, according to Hollywood legend, the report on Astaire's film test is supposed to have read, "Can't sing. Can't dance. Balding. Can dance a little." Astaire was a virtuoso dancer who was able to convey any emotion the dance called for. His technical control and sense of rhythm were astonishing. Astaire's execution of a dance routine was prized for its elegance, grace, originality, and precision. His perfection was legendary, and his artistry won him the admiration of such legendary twentieth-century dance legends as the Nicholas Brothers, Dame Margot Fonteyn, Gene Kelly, Bill "Bojangles" Robinson, and, of course, Gregory Hines.

One writer suggested that "it is the most difficult aspect of tap to master."

Hines is well known for experimenting with rhythm. In fact, he was one of the first tap dancers to radically alter one of the "rules" of tap dancing—that of keeping the same basic tempo throughout the routine. He recalled the first time he did it: "The first time I experimented with what I like to think of as 'No Time' was on the *Tonight Show*. I just decided to let it go. I was dancing in tempo, then I would stop in the step and go with a new tempo." Other dancers were upset at what seemed like a lapse; they even asked him if he had been drunk. "I took that as encouragement in a way," he recalled, "because up until that time, everybody was just saying, 'Boy, were you great! I just love that tap dancing!'" As far as Hines was concerned, he had presented a challenge, and that interested him.

Hines's style was enormously popular with audiences. He could be tough at one moment, slapping his feet hard on the floor, or smooth as he delicately glided over the stage. The tones and rhythms of his tapping shifted as he moved his lean, flexible body in imaginative flights across the floor, often breaking out of the classic 4/4 tempo of jazz. When Hines sang as he danced, audiences became intent on catching every word of his lyrics.

In the same unconventional style, Hines refused to use smiling as a performance tool. He seems to have felt this way even at a young age. He said that when he was a teenager, his family insisted that he smile while performing, just like all tap dancers of that time did, but he didn't want to. "The image always presented of the tap dancer is as happy, as smiling. It's always phony," he said. Consequently, Hines preferred to let the mood of the dance dictate whether he smiled or not. He explained that in his dancing, some steps might "give joy, connect me up with something," or there might be "a darkness to them. I hear a minor chord and I dance it." Sometimes, Hines grinned or shouted with pleasure, but generally, he danced with his head down, focusing on the sounds created by his tapping feet.

Almost everything about Hines's dancing was unconventional in terms of the history and rules of tap. Take a look at the style of Fred Astaire, for example. Astaire was probably the greatest movie dancer of his generation, but a viewer will immediately notice a big difference between the Hollywood style of tap dancing in the 1930s and 1940s that he exemplified and the newer, jazz-tap, improvisational style typified by artists like Gregory Hines. The smoothly elegant and graceful tapping of film stars such as Fred Astaire and Gene Kelly gave way in the 1970s to a newer, rougher, more urban style. This change of style was evident even in the dancer's choice of clothing: Astaire was famous for his top hat and tails, and Hines was known for dancing in tight sleeveless T-shirts and pleated, baggy trousers.

A journalist described Hines's well-known percussive style and how it differed from the stereotypical, smiling tap dancer in a tuxedo and top hat: "He taps hunkered over, bent at the waist, head cocked to the side, arms held loose, almost dangling. Although his feet play a range of sounds from delicate scrapes to fortissimo slaps, he seems to love it best when he is thwacking down the metal." Hines said that when he was hitting the floor, he wished that he "could bend far enough to get my ear right next to the floor and hear it stomp!" Hines's willingness, and his ability, to push the outer limits of what people expected from tap dancing made him one of the most popular and influential tap dancers of the late 1900s.

That resurgence in the popularity of tap dancing was still to come. During the 1960s, as rock and roll became more and more popular, tap dancing began to fade in popularity, appearing old-fashioned in comparison. Along with tap's declining popularity, fewer people were learning to tap dance during the 1950s and 1960s: There was something of a "tap drought." In an effort to stay popular, the Hines, Hines and Dad act began to add more comedy and jazz music to its routines, reflecting what they hoped audiences wanted to see.

On a more personal level, other changes were taking place as well. Gregory was discovering women. During a stint at a resort in the Catskills (a mountainous resort area northwest of New York City, where many entertainers got their start) in the late 1960s, Gregory's mother visited every weekend to do her son's laundry. One weekday, however, Hines was lured into the laundry room by a bunch of guys who told him that a group of young women were in the room. Hines described it later: "It was a great meeting place! The girls were showing me how to fold. It was the first independent thing I'd done away from my mother, and it felt good."

One of the girls he met in the Catskills was a dance therapist named Patricia Panella. Hines, who was 22 years old at the time, felt the need to establish his own identity separate from his family, so in 1968, he married Patricia. They made their home in New York City and, in 1971, had a daughter, Daria. Within a couple of years, however, then-27-year-old Gregory realized that creating his own family wasn't enough—he no longer wanted to work with his brother and father. He later confided: "I knew I didn't want to work with the family, which was traumatic." The life he had led since he was just a little boy was about to be irrevocably altered.

4

An Ending and a New Beginning

By 1972, it seemed that Gregory Hines had everything to look forward to. He was enjoying a promising and successful career, a close family, a wife, and a young daughter—even a dog. He was also, he said later, desperately unhappy. For almost 25 years, he had tapped his way across the United States and Europe with his brother and father, part of a routine act that left him feeling trapped and unsatisfied. For Hines, the tedious travel from one unfulfilling job to another was beginning to overwhelm him. He tried self-medicating—using the illegal drug cocaine to try to escape his sense of unhappiness. Years later, he commented that "it took about a year for my nose and sinuses to come back" after he stopped using the drug.

He and his brother were also at odds with each other and growing apart. The years of performing together had taken their toll. Hines wanted to try his hand at songwriting and become a rock musician. His brother's ambition was to pursue acting and perfomance theater. Things between the two got so bad that one time, while on tour in San Francisco, Hines avoided talking to brother Maurice by crossing to the other side of the street. Shortly thereafter, when they had a fight that nearly ended in blows, Hines knew the partnership was over.

Hines was ready to break free from the family act, but that alone was not enough to ease his dissatisfaction with his life. His marriage was falling apart as well. Later, he recalled the painful memory of deciding to break away. He was sitting in his kitchen thinking about what to do when Gladys Knight's song "Neither One of Us (Wants to Be the First to Say Goodbye)" started playing on the radio. When he heard the line *Farewell, my love*, he broke down in tears. "[Knight] was talking about my life. She was just talking to me."

So, wrenching though it was, Hines told his family that he was through with the act and with his marriage. In 1973, with no job, no money, and no real plans, Hines moved from New York City to Venice, California. There he founded a jazz-rock band called Severance—supposedly with the help of a $5,000 loan from entertainer Bill Cosby. The band was far from successful. "On a really great week in Venice in five years, I made $40," Hines recalled years later.

During his time in Venice, Hines earned a black belt in karate and probably could have made a decent living teaching the art if that was what he had wanted. Instead, he eked out a living by playing and singing in bars around Los Angeles, writing songs, and even occasionally working as a busboy. Although Hines often said that he did not remember a time when he was not dancing, he also admitted that during this period, he "didn't even own a pair of dance shoes." It seems that he wanted to make a clean break from anything in his past—including tap dancing. In an interview in 1986, Hines said,

I didn't choose to be in the business. I don't remember not dancing. I could always do it. When I got to be about twenty-five, I became very disenchanted. . . . I got interested in the music of the time. I started smokin' dope, I started drinking, I started slowing down and trying to find myself. I didn't want to work in nightclubs. I didn't want to do *Fiddler on the Roof* medleys. I didn't know what I wanted to do. I just knew I was miserable.

Hines was also lonely. He admitted that he "was just so scared of being alone" that he would say anything to a female companion to keep from having to go home and be by himself. At the same time, he took advantage of the so-called hippie lifestyle and its free-and-easy attitude toward the use of illegal drugs. "Venice Beach was a real charged atmosphere then. It was music, women, and drugs, and I had my share of all three," Hines said. Once, when his mother called him from New York, he told her, "Look, I just dropped some acid [LSD—a powerful hallucinogenic drug], so I can't talk now." He also indulged in less dangerous excitements, such as having his ear pierced, at a time when very few men would even think of such a thing.

In Venice, Hines met Pamela Koslow, the woman who would help him overcome his loneliness and eventually become his second wife. Pamela was from a respectable middle-class Jewish family and had grown up on New York City's Upper East Side. She had attended the prestigious Bronx High School of Science, gone on to City College, and then studied at the University of California at Los Angeles for a second degree. She became a student counselor and married an economics professor, who seemed the proper choice of husband for a woman of her background.

Like Hines, however, Koslow was desperately unhappy. She found herself boxed in and stifled, trapped in a life and marriage that left her feeling unsatisfied, even though it seemed

Gregory Hines met Pamela Koslow (left) in Venice, California. Both Hines and Koslow were going through difficult times in their lives and found solace in each other's company. Koslow encouraged Hines to "do what you want to do." He found her outlook refreshing.

the correct thing to do. The cultural atmosphere in Los Angeles was far from that of her traditional upbringing on New York's Upper East Side. Because of this, she could readily understand and relate to the similar feelings that led Hines to move to California.

Neither she nor Hines had any real goals when they met. Koslow was recently divorced and struggling to raise her daughter, Jessica. She was, however, determined not to continue her job counseling students for the simple reason that she had no faith in the very goals she would have to tell students to set. Her philosophy became "Do what you want to do," and she told Hines, "If you feel like doing nothing, then that's just what you should do." Hines responded immediately. "Here, for the first time," he said later, "was someone who was letting me be me. There were no pressures."

Doing nothing, "being me," and living without pressures, however, did not bring in a whole lot of money. At first, Pamela was able to support Hines. He recalled that "she would pay my rent, take me out to dinner and buy shoes for Daria." Then he added with a laugh, "She used to tell me she felt she was a patron of the arts." When the money began to run out, Koslow was forced to peddle pottery, clothing, and other goods along the beach in Venice. Hines occupied himself writing songs that nobody wanted to hear.

When his divorce from Patricia was finalized, Hines was granted visitation rights with Daria. With the live-for-the-moment lifestyle he was leading in California, he could not give her the kind of home he wanted her to have. The first time Daria came to visit from New York, Hines had no place for them to stay. They ended up moving from house to house on the beach, camping out with various friends of Hines's and Koslow's. Embarrassed by his circumstances and afraid that Daria would not be allowed further visits, he asked her not to tell her mother. The little girl responded, "Whenever we crash, can you make sure the people have a TV?" Father and daughter kept their promises to each other.

Aware of his daughter's need for him and of his own desire to be a better parent, Hines joined a group for single fathers. "I had to join them," he said later, "because I love my daughter and I didn't want to make too many mistakes in raising her. Besides, I didn't want to inadvertently put all my attitudes, my hang-ups, on her." It was a challenge, but as Hines said, "It was fabulous. I felt like I was really learning how to be a father. I discovered the joy of single parenting."

At the same time, Hines also joined a group of men who met to discuss how men treat women. He did it, he explained, to free himself of the burden men often feel about relation-ships with women, and the fear they have of openly expressing their feelings. Thanks to his involvement in these groups and with the love and support of Koslow, Hines began to free him-self from his fears and insecurities.

There was no question in Hines's mind that the Venice period strengthened him by giving him the time to evaluate his situation. He explained:

> I think everybody at some point—especially if they've been working their whole lives—should take time out and think about what they've done. That period of reflection meant a lot to me. I grew up a lot. With the family, I always had a buf-fer. After a while, I didn't know how to take care of myself. I was twenty-seven years old and very immature. During that period in Venice, I found out how to take care of myself.

The time in Venice may have helped Hines grow up, but he realized that he could not spend his life there. He didn't really have a career. His band had performed some club dates and had even released an album, but it had failed. In 1977, the band broke up, and Hines got a job giving guitar lessons. He was rejected for a job as a songwriter for Warner Brothers. Most importantly, he missed his daughter, and he wanted to move back to New York to be closer to her. One day, he and Koslow discovered they had just $10 between them. It was time to leave Venice behind.

What would he do in New York to support himself and his family? He thought he might give guitar lessons or teach karate, but his brother, Maurice Hines Jr. had other ideas. At that time, Maurice was set for a spot in the road show of the musical *Pippin*. He told Gregory there was plenty of work in New York for tap dancers, and because he would be touring out of town with *Pippin,* he offered Gregory the use of his apartment.

When Gregory Hines and Pamela Koslow arrived in New York, Maurice was not out on the road. He had quit the show after a disagreement with the director. Fortunately for Gregory, though, Maurice had persuaded his agent to submit Hines's name to audition for a play called *The Last Minstrel Show*. Hines described what happened:

> When I auditioned for [*The Last Minstrel Show*], the agent said, "Yeah, you got it, and they've offered $650 a week, but that's not good enough. I'm going to try to get $750 and get your name in a box." I said, "Are you kidding? I don't care about $750, I don't care about a box. I just want this job. Man, if you blow this for me, I'm going to tear your office apart." But he did get $750 and my name in a box.

For the first time in years, Hines was back onstage.

Hines was in his element again, tapping and playing drums. Of his comeback, he says: "I hadn't had my tap shoes on for eight years . . . from the time I started back tapping, because of the experience in Venice, I was a different person. It was the first time I felt I had something I wanted to say." *The Last Minstrel Show* closed in Philadelphia without ever opening on Broadway, but Hines's next show would be more successful.

EUBIE!

Hines appeared next in *Eubie!*, along with his brother Maurice. Choreographed by their old teacher and mentor, Henry LeTang, *Eubie!* was a musical revue based on the songs of pianist and composer Eubie Blake. Blake was a legendary African-American composer and pianist of ragtime, jazz, and popular music, whose career spanned nearly the length of the twentieth century.

For Hines, getting the role was not all that easy. After his audition, he was certain he had gotten the job, but much to his surprise, he was turned down. "There must be some mis-

Eubie! was a musical revue based on the songs of pianist and composer Eubie Blake. Hines's old teacher, Henry LeTang, choreographed the show, and Hines appeared in the show along with his brother, Maurice. Gregory Hines was nominated for a Tony Award for his performance. Above, from left to right: Maurice Hines, Gregory Hines, and Lonnie McNeil perform in the show.

take," he told the producer, "I was great at the audition. You've got to give me another audition." After many phone calls, the producer agreed. On the second day of rehearsal, Hines was informed that he had the role. His persistence had paid off. To add to Hines's self-confidence, and to his professional credit, he received a Tony nomination for Best Featured Actor in a Musical for his performance in *Eubie!*. The Tony Awards are given annually as recognition of excellence in theater and are considered Broadway's top award, the equivalent of the Academy Award for film. Hines was thrilled to receive the nomination, but he did not win, losing to Henderson Forsythe in the musical *The Best Little Whorehouse in Texas*.

Despite the loss, from that point on, Gregory Hines's career was in full swing. In a later interview, he emphasized that he did not return to New York with a desire to get back into show business. Instead, he got back into performing because he found himself in New York with only $40 in his pocket and no other prospects. "To this day I think if I had had three days to consider it [whether to audition], I might have said 'I'd rather not.'"

Whatever the reason for taking up his career again, Hines had learned something from getting the part in *Eubie!*: Persistence pays off. From then on he would be, as he put it, persistent just short of being obnoxious. His time away from show business had also liberated him as a dancer, allowing him to realize that he could perform the way he wanted to perform. It pushed him toward what he really wanted to do, and his determination to do what he wanted made him aggressive enough to succeed—twice!—in the tough world of New York show business. Hines's Broadway performances earned him rave reviews and the attention of entertainment professionals who knew a star when they saw one.

5

Human Lightning

Hines's first few years back in New York were filled with his new-found Broadway career. At first, it was difficult for him to begin tapping again. During his years in Venice, he had lost some of his physical fitness and resilience. He quickly adjusted to the rigorous exercise, however, and he knew he had finally found what he wanted to do.

Reviewers fell in love with Gregory Hines. Although *The Last Minstrel Show* was a box-office disappointment, Hines himself was praised for his performance. During the successful run of *Eubie!*, which opened on Broadway in May 1978, both Gregory and Maurice Hines earned rave reviews. Influential critic Brendan Gill of *New Yorker* magazine singled out the duo in his review of the show: "The Hines brothers are especially to be praised for their whirling-dervish-like dancing."

Hines's next show, the musical *Comin' Uptown*, opened in November 1979. It was an all-black version of Dickens's *A*

Christmas Carol, in which Hines played Scrooge. The play was
not particularly well received; in fact, it was a monumental flop,
playing only 45 performances. One critic who panned the show
for its writing and songs did praise Hines's performance, however. Commenting that the only reason to see the play was Gregory Hines, he went on to write: "He is a marvelous performer,
with an inhumanly agile body and a joie de vivre that appears
to be more than mere professional [makeup]." Another reviewer
urged audiences to see Hines in the role, praising the dancer's
agility and wit and his seeming defiance of the laws of gravity
as his tapping feet express "the entire spectrum of comedy, from
smiles to belly laughs, into ecstatic movement." Hines earned a
second Tony nomination, this time in the category of Best Performance by a Leading Actor in a Musical, for his performance
in *Comin' Uptown.* Unfortunately, he lost, for the second year in
a row, this time to Jim Dale in the musical *Barnum.*

Hines, despite the failure of *Comin' Uptown,* was not going
to be unemployed for long. In 1980, he appeared in the show
Black Broadway, which traced the hits of black musicians and
performers throughout the first half of the twentieth century.
The real stars of the play, though, were the great performers
from the past, including such greats as tap dancer John W.
Bubbles of the famous duo Buck and Bubbles. Hines appeared
with his contemporary Nell Carter (from the Tony Award winning musical *Ain't Misbehavin'*), and together they represented
present-day black Broadway. A reviewer characterized Hines as
"a one-man funky fusillade."

In February 1981, Hines opened in the Broadway smash
Sophisticated Ladies, a revue of the great composer Duke
Ellington's music. Hines exulted in his role, putting what he
felt were his true talents on display for the first time. "This
was jazz!" he proclaimed. "This was Duke Ellington! We had
so much fun. . . . We jumped every night. It really was the first
time I was seen by the public, the first time I really had an
opportunity to do the things I can do."

Although Hines's costar was the classically trained modern dancer Judith Jamison, a living legend for her performances with the Alvin Ailey American Dance Theater, it was Hines who won the accolades. *New York Times* critic Frank Rich wrote, "This man is human lightning and he just can't be contained." According to *New York* magazine, Hines was not only talented at dancing, singing, acting, and even drumming but was "also a redolent personality, a pervasive mood that saturates the stage with whimsy." The same reviewer declared that Hines's "tapping seems to sing even more than dance."

In *Time* magazine, Gerald Clarke added to the praise, saying,

> Slim and rakish, Hines wields the fastest pair of spats in the East; his feet move with percussive force. In the show's most exciting number, "Kinda Dukish," Hines recalls Bojangles' famous stair routine, tapping his way up a flight and then, with audacious nonchalance, tapping back down again—accompanied by cheers from the audience. "His feet are going 150 miles an hour," says [Judith] Jamison.

Duke Ellington

Edward Kennedy "Duke" Ellington (April 29, 1899–May 24, 1974) was an American jazz composer, pianist, and band leader who has been called one of the most influential figures in jazz, if not in all of American music.

A stylish, suave, elegant man, Ellington preferred to call his style and sound "American music" rather than just jazz. Best known for such songs as "Mood Indigo," "Sophisticated Lady," "Satin Doll," and "It Don't Mean a Thing (If It Ain't Got That Swing)," he is also respected for his efforts to extend jazz beyond the three-minute song with pieces such as "Black, Brown, and Beige," "Diminuendo and Crescendo in Blue," "Harlem," and for his concerts of sacred music.

Awarded the Grammy Lifetime Achievement Award in 1966, Duke Ellington went on to receive the Presidential Medal of Freedom in 1969 and the Legion of Honor by France in 1973, the highest civilian honors in each country. His influence on music was enormous.

Indeed, *Sophisticated Ladies* was an ideal showcase for Hines's talents as an actor, dancer, and singer, further solidifying his reputation as one of Broadway's most talented stars, and for this he was rewarded with his third Tony nomination. For the third year in a row, he failed to win the award, losing to Kevin Klein for his performance in Gilbert and Sullivan's *The Pirates of Penzance*.

Although he loved performing in the show, Hines wanted to move on to other projects. After a year in the play, he left, and his brother Maurice replaced him.

In 1981, during the run of *Sophisticated Ladies*, Hines and his longtime love, Pam Koslow, were married. Of their relationship, Hines had said, "This love that we have, it is the most powerful emotion in my life." He expressed his contentment and security in his marriage when he added, "I don't know what it is with Pamela and me but I am never completely comfortable when I'm not around her." Two years later, the couple had a son, Zachary.

Being married to a star has its difficulties. A common question asked of celebrity spouses is whether they feel jealous that their performing spouse does love scenes with other actors—actors who are often sex symbols themselves. Koslow, for one, said that she had "gotten used to" her husband's willingness to do love scenes in his movies and shows. Hines was, she said, "a loving, physical man," and she acknowledged that that "is the kind of image he wants to portray to young African-American men."

One particular difficulty the couple had to overcome was the reaction of some to an interracial marriage. Before their marriage, Koslow's parents were not entirely thrilled with the match. They finally came to accept their daughter's choice, however, just as Hines's own grandfather had to learn to accept Hines's mother's choice, many years before.

Hines has said that in the 1960s, when he was dating Pat Panella, his first wife, people on the street would occasionally

Gregory Hines and Pamela Koslow married in 1981 and had a son, Zachary, in 1983. Above, Hines poses with Zach at the premiere of the movie *The Peacemaker.* Hines also had a daughter, Daria, from his previous marriage.

stare at the racially mixed couple. (It's interesting to note that it wasn't until 1967 that the U.S. Supreme Court struck down all state laws regarding miscegenation—interracial marriage—throughout the United States, finally making it legal for blacks and whites to marry in any state of the union.) Later, as social tensions eased because of the freer attitudes of the late 1960s and 1970s, Hines noticed a marked change, a decrease in negative attention. As for his own feelings about his current marriage, he said, "If someone didn't really particularly care for my choice, I have never felt that I needed to explain or justify it because my love for Pamela has always felt so right. From the time I met her, it just felt like we should be together. So any kind of energy that I have ever felt that people didn't particularly dig it usually passed by me pretty quickly."

Hines was never one for whom difficulty was a serious obstacle. Based on his life and the career choices he made, it seemed obvious that he would do whatever was necessary to express himself, both as a person and an artist. The stubborn determination to succeed and be happy doing it was one of his strongest virtues.

Throughout the 1980s, Hines's career opportunities and personal life were gathering steam, and he continued to perform onstage. In 1985, he began touring, and for two years, traveled and performed live as a soloist. He wanted to continue honing his dance skills without being confined by the structure of a musical play. It was then that his signature style of improvisational jazz tap dancing truly came into its own. "I really began to develop," he remembered, "because I sometimes had to dance every night. I was pressed to improvise. I had to come up with stuff. And I had to relax and not push."

A major problem for tap dancers is the quality of the surface on which they perform, which affects the sound of the tap. Hines and his manager, John Shivers, attacked this never-ending problem while on tour. The two created a portable stage that could travel easily but still be an excellent percussive instrument. Made of oak, the floor was equipped with especially sensitive microphones that picked up the sounds of Hines's feet. He was appearing with musicians who played electronic instruments, so, Hines explained, "I couldn't pound out the whole dance every night. In order to be subtle, to be able to place my foot down softly and pull it 'sh-shush,' and still have the audience hear it, the sound had to be loud."

Frequently, when performers become successful, their attitudes and behavior change, and the transformation is not always for the better. Hines was aware of this and made a conscious effort to stay grounded. "I'm not sure it's healthy for me to talk about myself so much," he once told an interviewer. "There's so much that's unhealthy in this business. I saw it when I did *Sophisticated Ladies.* . . . 'I did this, I did that, me me me.' I'd come home and want to talk about myself some more." Fortunately for Hines, Koslow knew how to bring him back down to earth: "My wife said 'Okay, Mr. Broadway Star, take down the garbage.' And, you know, I respected that."

By the mid 1980s, the husband who carried out the trash was also "Mr. Broadway Star." Gregory Hines had proved that hard work, persistence, and dedication to his craft could culminate in success. It was not just fame on Broadway, however. Hines would also prove that his talents could conquer the tough world of Hollywood, a world where blacks have largely been second-class citizens.

6

The Tough World
of Hollywood

Assertiveness is a necessity for black artists in the film industry, and it was particularly important for Hines when he was trying to break into Hollywood. Minority men and women were often at a disadvantage, with their opportunities largely limited to playing stereotypical roles. With the premiere of director Spike Lee's successful *She's Gotta Have It* in 1986, what had been a limited playing field for black film professionals began to show signs of change.

The film, made in just 12 days for the phenomenally low cost of $175,000, featured a female lead character who was black, young, attractive, and confident, trying to choose between three very different suitors. Ultimately earning more than $7 million, the movie made Spike Lee a filmmaker to be reckoned with and earned glowing reviews. The *New York Times* wrote that *She's Gotta Have It* was "a groundbreaking film for African-American filmmakers and a welcome change

When Gregory Hines was trying to break into Hollywood, respectable roles for minority men and women were few and far between. Things began to change in 1986, when director Spike Lee's first movie, *She's Gotta Have It*, was released. Above, Spike Lee listens to the star of his movie, Tracy Camilla Johns, at a release party for the film.

in the representation of blacks in American cinema, depicting men and women of color not as pimps and whores, but as intelligent, upscale urbanites."

The changed opportunities were more the result of the growth of independent filmmakers, the "indies," who usually completed and distributed their work outside the studio-controlled industry based in Hollywood. Relatively few African Americans and other minorities work within the studio system, although such box-office stars as Denzel Washington,

Halle Berry, and Will Smith have shown the major studios that black actors can appeal to white audiences.

This is not to say that African Americans have not played their part in the history of American film. Black filmmaker Oliver Micheaux, whose independent career spanned the decades from the 1920s through the 1940s, broke the color line fairly early in the history of movies, although his films were marketed nearly exclusively to black audiences. Actors such as Stepin Fetchit (the first black actor to receive star billing), Hattie McDaniel (the first black actor, male or female, to win an Oscar), and Bill "Bojangles" Robinson were able to perform within the confines of the Hollywood system. Nevertheless, these talented entertainers were generally relegated to stereotypical roles in white mainstream films.

There is a story about Hattie McDaniel, who won her Oscar in 1939 for Best Supporting Actress as Scarlett O'Hara's mammy in *Gone with the Wind*. McDaniel often portrayed maids in films and was sometimes criticized by African Americans for accepting these roles. She is said to have responded to her critics by pointing out that she could be a maid for seven dollars a week or she could play a maid for $700 a week. The choice seemed obvious.

Parts for blacks in films were written to appeal to white audiences, not to portray blacks as they actually viewed themselves. Blacks in films were portrayed as caricatures of the way whites saw them. Most young black filmgoers could not recognize real black people in the characters portrayed in film.

An exception to this rule took place during the 1950s and 1960s, in the persona of the elegant Sidney Poitier. Poitier, handsome and every inch a star, starred in such classic films as *The Defiant Ones, A Raisin in the Sun, Lilies of the Field, In the Heat of the Night,* and *Guess Who's Coming to Dinner.* Playing roles that defied traditional racial stereotypes,

Poitier's sheer force of talent made him as popular with white audiences as he was with black. Harry Belafonte, too, was a popular African-American film star who appealed to a broad mainstream audience.

Other than these two talented actors, very few black role models appeared in films in the post–World War II period. When a young and impressionable Gregory Hines was tap dancing his way through nightclubs with his brother and admiring the black performers he met backstage, few African-American actors played on the big screen or on television. Blacks were, in some ways, nearly invisible.

By the late 1960s, however, in the midst of the civil rights and black power movements, many African Americans, who had once embraced Sidney Poitier as a positive role model, now criticized his roles as "sterile" or "middle class." Like young Gregory Hines, most blacks wanted portrayals more "real" and more three-dimensional than the characters Poitier portrayed.

CHANGES IN HOLLYWOOD

The skyrocketing popularity of television in the 1950s and 1960s, coupled with a corresponding decrease in movie ticket sales, threw Hollywood studios into a financial crisis. This situation, combined with the societal changes brought on by World War II and its aftermath and the black liberation movements, compelled the nearly all-white studio heads to change the film industry. It was essential to draw viewers into theaters, and black audiences were increasingly vocal in demanding more realistic portrayals of African Americans.

Gordon Parks Sr. became the first black director of a major studio film, *The Learning Tree*, for Warner Brothers Studios in 1969. Parks described the experience:

> I had fourteen or fifteen [black] people behind the camera
> for the first time in the history of films. There was a black
> director. The producer was black. The scoring was done by

a black man. The third cameraman for the first time was a black man. . . . The minute [Kenny Hyman of Warner Brothers] did it, everybody felt "well, it's happened. We better open up now."

According to Parks, all it takes for change to occur is for people in positions of power in the film industry to make a commitment to diversity.

Following *The Learning Tree*, the independent filmmaker Melvin Van Peebles raised money and produced the 1970 release *Sweet Sweetback's Baad Asssss Song*. As one film historian commented, Van Peebles's film single-handedly "changed the course of African American film production and the depiction of African Americans on screen." This film, along with the films *Shaft* (1971, directed by Parks) and *Superfly* (1972, directed by Parks's son Gordon Parks Jr.), ushered in the era of the so-called "blaxploitation" films. The term, coined by the industry publication *Variety*, refers to the usually poorly made films that stereotyped blacks as aggressive, often violent, characters. Unlike *Sweetback*, *Shaft*, and *Superfly*, however, the films that introduced the genre, later blaxploitation films were usually written, directed, and distributed by whites, who were merely exploiting an audience's need to see black characters on the screen.

The idea behind blaxploitation films continued the tradition of African American folk tales like Br'er Rabbit and John Henry, in which the hero outsmarts authority figures. Since sex, violence, and drugs were often the themes of these films, they have been characterized as the "bad black man" tradition. In *Sweetback*, the main character is a hustler on the run who is protected by the black community. This was obviously a very different role from the noble characters that Poitier and Belafonte often played. The increasing visibility of African-American film professionals—on the screen and behind it—was beginning to reflect the change from white-produced films targeted to white audiences.

Despite increasing exposure for black actors, blaxploitation films still represented the white view of blacks. Gregory Hines noted that the roles for black men in blaxploitation films were just as limiting (and stereotypical) in their own way as were the earlier sterilized roles. Hines consistently emphasized that African Americans must be portrayed as three-dimensional characters.

Nevertheless, even during blaxploitation's heyday in the 1970s, realistic films for black audiences were being produced by other filmmakers, among them Harry Belafonte, Ossie Davis, and black-owned distribution companies such as TAM and Cinematics International. Sidney Poitier, too, was still a powerful influence in white Hollywood. When the era of blaxploitation films ended around 1974, these artists and companies continued to produce films that shattered the movie stereotype of African Americans.

By the time Gregory Hines broke into films in the early 1980s, Hollywood was producing yet another kind of film. While Hines was getting his career back on track, accruing Broadway credits and starting to make films, Hollywood was discovering the financial goldmine of the blockbuster film. This was the age of *Star Wars*, *Jaws*, and Indiana Jones. Rather than make unique films that appeal to selected audiences, Hollywood invested monumental sums of money in films calculated to have the widest possible audience appeal. Again, African-American film professionals found that they were mostly ignored by Hollywood.

It's true that actors like Richard Pryor and Eddie Murphy did become superstars in white-produced, mostly white-cast films, pulling in a sizable African-American audience. Aside from these two stars, however, Hollywood still offered few real opportunities for blacks.

According to Gregory Hines, it is essential, particularly for black artists, to be aggressive in going after what they want. He for one never shied away from aggressively pursuing his film goals, which was to take any good role regardless of whether the character as written was supposed to be white or black. Describing how he got the role in the 1986 film *Running Scared*, he explained his method:

> I read the script, and I knew it was a good part. It was written for a white actor. That's what I'm up against—I have to try to make roles happen for me that aren't written black. The roles written black are the "cool guys," and I don't want to play the cool guy. . . . It's incumbent upon me to go after things, because nobody's going to say "Why are we just looking at white actors? Let's look at everybody." They never do that. . . .

Many film professionals believe that the lack of obvious opportunities for minorities is the result of and a perpetuation of racism in America. It is important to note, however, that the film industry is a business just like any other; Hollywood is designed to sell product and make money. The budgets for blockbuster films, including mass-marketing strategies, are so enormous that the films must draw in as many people as possible just for the studio to break even, let alone make a profit. Without profits, studios are even less willing than usual to consider producing modest projects that appeal to smaller audiences—and thus bring in lower profits. Films targeted to a mass audience simply take into account the fact that the majority of that audience is white and assume that, therefore, that audience prefers to see white actors rather than black.

Yaphet Kotto, a black actor who has played significant roles in Hollywood-produced films, agrees, concluding that the situation is based on economics, not racism. "People want to be involved in fifteen- to twenty-million-dollar movies, and they want their returns guaranteed," he said. "So they go for the Redfords, the Connerys, the Brandos . . . if they ever scale their expectations down and return to modest, low-budget films, they might just turn to me."

Whatever the reason, the statistics show that Hollywood has traditionally been closed to all but a very few minority men and women. In 1969, 40 percent of the Los Angeles metropolitan area population were minorities, but minorities comprised only 3 percent of the film industry's labor force. In the 1980s, the situation remained largely unchanged. Litigation and the threat of a boycott by the National Association for the Advancement of Colored People (NAACP) and other organizations exposed the fact that very few minorities (especially minority women) were being hired at the major studios. Only one-tenth of the 50 black-directed theatrical films were done by women, and the first was in 1991 (*Daughters in the Dust*, directed by Julie Dash). In 1991, out of 450 studio and major independent releases, only 12 were directed by black men; none was directed by black women. (Dash produced and released her film completely outside the studio system.)

Film industry insiders claim that getting jobs in the film industry depends on "who you know." Since nearly all of the power positions in Hollywood are still held by white males, their white male acquaintances and business associates are more likely than minorities to get a foot in the door. Minorities are then at a disadvantage because they do not hear about potential jobs in a word-of-mouth recruiting system. Gregory Hines was quite aware of this system. He himself had been cast in shows or movies in which he knew the producer, director, or another influential person—for example, the movies *Wolfen* and *Running Scared*.

Still, several successful films released in the 1990s, which featured story lines relevant to the African-American experience, have proved that there is an audience demand for films that are not all "lily-white." Movies such as *The Preacher's Wife*, *A Rage in Harlem*, and *Waiting to Exhale* (all of which Hines appeared in) helped prove to Hollywood that profits can be made by increasing minority roles in films.

Hines himself believed things were changing, as he explained: "Besides developing roles for black actors, producers and directors are starting to realize, Hey, we don't have to write 'black' dialogue; just hire a black actor and say, 'Make it you.' The day is gone when every black man has to be 'Yeah, man, I dig it.' I mean, black people also say, 'Yes, I understand.'"

Hines's own film career stands as proof of his belief. Any artist as talented and determined as Hines is bound to break out of the expected track and forge his own career whether on stage, in films, or in television.

7

Gregory Hines, Movie Star

Unlike his first break on Broadway, Hines's early film auditions were anything but romantic movie material. "I read for a basketball movie called *The Fish That Saved Pittsburgh*, and a movie that was never released called *House of God*," he recalled. Despite being rejected, the aspiring film actor stuck with it, knowing it was something he was eager to try.

Gregory had also had some encouragement from another highly regarded actor. Years earlier, before he had dropped out and gone to California, Hines had been spotted by actor Dustin Hoffman during one of his shows at the Plaza Hotel's Persian Room in New York City. At that time, Hoffman encouraged Hines to seek a film career, telling the dancer he thought he had ability as an actor.

Nothing comes easily, however. In show business, much of a person's success or lack of it has to do with timing. About two years after the Persian Room meeting, when Hoffman was looking for Hines for a film project, the dancer was in Venice, California, out of contact and out of show business, at least for the time being.

Once Hines was back in the entertainment field, he knew that film was something he wanted to try. "I wanted to make a movie," Hines said. "The whole life of the movies appealed to me. You work hard for three or four months, then you don't work at all for a couple of months. I also like the idea of doing a movie, then doing a play, couple of movies, then a play. Also, [unlike a play] if you do a movie, you can go see it."

Doing live stage work is transient and of the moment, something dancers and stage actors must get used to, but for the stage performer, being able to see one's own work is a treat. "I love it," he said of making movies. "I love the environment. I love the collaborative excitement. And I love making something that can last. Most of my life I have been doing things that, once done, they disappear."

In 1981, as Hines was getting used to consistent work on Broadway and was building a life with his new wife, the beginnings of a film career opened up. He was tapped for a role in the film *Wolfen*, whose lead was Albert Finney. About his film debut, Hines said that it was "the first time I ever did any kind of a [show business] job where I didn't dance."

Although Hines may have missed a chance to work with Dustin Hoffman by being out of circulation, he still had important connections. His first film role, as a medical examiner in *Wolfen*, came to him in part because he knew the film's director "from when we were hippies together." Talent and skill as a stage performer is not the same thing as performing in movies, however. Hines still had to learn to act for films. He described how it worked:

> I think sometimes Albert [Finney] would just look at me- just before we would have to go through a doorway, when the cameras were running—and realize I had nothing on

my mind except the words I was trying to remember. Sometimes he would just suggest something: "If I were you, I
would want to be a little somber when I came through that
door." And suddenly a light bulb would go off in my head—
he would make the words mean something.

Although Hines's character did not survive the end of the
film (he was devoured by wolves halfway through), Hines
obviously learned a great deal about acting from the experience. His aptitude for the craft of film acting only increased
with each film he participated in. Over the years Hines's development as an actor contributed greatly to his attractiveness as
a property, encouraging producers and directors to cast him
in nondancing as well as dancing roles. His star power also
helped to ensure backing. As a well-known talent, his name on
a project could command the financing needed to make the
films. Ironically, after years of working on Broadway, Hines is
probably best remembered as a film and television actor by his
many fans.

It is not just Hines's acting skills that were in demand for
films, however. The 1984 film *The Cotton Club* gave him the
opportunity to combine his formidable dancing skills with
his talent as an actor. In the film, Hines portrayed tap dancer
William Sandman, one-half of a tapping duo. His brother,
Maurice Jr., was cast as his partner. Hines characterized *The
Cotton Club* as "The big return of dance to the screen. . . . It
was only a matter of time before people would want to see
dance in movies." Unlike other dance films of the period, such
as *Flashdance, Saturday Night Fever*, and *Dirty Dancing, The
Cotton Club* was a film about old-fashioned tap dancing.

The movie *The Cotton Club* was based on the famous
New York City nightclub of the same name that operated in
Harlem during the 1920s and 1930s. Performers there had
included many of the greatest African-American entertainers of the era, including Duke Ellington, Cab Calloway, Louis

The Cotton Club, directed by the legendary Francis Ford Coppola, intrigued Gregory Hines from the very start. The producer, Robert Evans, wanted Hines to play the role of Cab Calloway, while Hines wanted to star as Sandman Williams. Hines got his way, and he is shown here as Williams with costar Lonette McKee as Lila Rose Oliver.

Armstrong, Ethel Waters, Lena Horne, and tap dancers Bill "Bojangles" Robinson and the Nicholas Brothers. Ironically, they performed for largely white audiences; blacks were generally denied admission to the club. During that time, it became trendy for rich whites to make the trek up to Harlem and experience the exotic world of African-American culture and nightlife.

To make his movie, the film's director, Francis Ford Coppola, assembled an impressive cast of tap dancers, which included Henry LeTang and Charles "Honi" Coles, the legendary soft-shoe tapper, as well as brothers Gregory and Maurice

Hines. It was, obviously, an extraordinary lineup of dancers, and Gregory Hines was excited about making the film.

Hines particularly liked working with Coppola. The director thoroughly researched the historical background, going through endless period footage of tap dancing. Coppola carefully videotaped all rehearsals, yet allowed for improvisation, an approach that strongly appealed to Hines. "He [Coppola] sets up situations," Hines explained, "then lets you improvise. He's like a jazz musician, he's so sensitive."

In the film, Hines's character, William, breaks up the act with his brother, just as Hines did in real life. In their real life, the two brothers were no longer close. Hines attributed much of this to the fact that he and Maurice were two very different people. He also blamed sibling rivalry combined with professional jealousy because they both worked in the same profession. "So much of our relationship was the act,"

Maurice Hines Jr.

Although he often seemed to live in the shadow of his more famous brother, Maurice Hines Jr. has had a distinguished career in his own right.

After the family act of Hines, Hines and Dad broke up, Maurice went out on his own, starring as Nathan Detroit in the national tour of *Guys and Dolls*. He also starred on Broadway in *Eubie!*, *Bring Back Birdie*, *Sophisticated Ladies*, and *Uptown . . . It's Hot!*, which he also choreographed, earning a Tony Award nomination as Best Actor in a Musical in the process, and *Hot Feet*, which he conceived, choreographed, and directed.

Hines codirected and choreographed the national tour of the Louis Armstrong musical biography *Satchmo* and directed, choreographed, and starred in the national tour of *Harlem Suite*. He directed and choreographed *Havana Night* in Cuba and an all-Latino production of *The Red Shoes* in the Dominican Republic. He also created the revue *Broadway Soul Jam* to inaugurate an entertainment complex in Holland.

The first African American to direct at Radio City Music Hall, Hines is currently at work on *Yo Alice*, an urban hip-hop fantasy he conceived and will direct and choreograph.

In the film *The Cotton Club*, Gregory (right) and Maurice Hines played brothers who start out as dance partners but eventually split up. The scene was painful for the two brothers to play because they had experienced a very similar rift in their own lives.

Gregory explained. "And maybe with my brother and me, the act might have been what kept us together [when the brothers were children]. And when it was gone, it was tough for us to find a reason to spend time together."

Maurice saw their relationship somewhat differently. He certainly acknowledged that Gregory was immensely talented but added that his brother "knows how to play the system." He also went on to criticize Gregory for the roles he played in black revues. Maurice insisted that his own true interest was in the legitimate theater and not in redoing black shows. Maurice also contended that his brother made professional compromises throughout his career. He illustrated his point by citing a role Hines played in the Mel Brooks film *History of the World, Part I,* in which he portrayed a slave. That, said Maurice, was a part he would never have accepted.

Despite the antagonisms, when Gregory Hines was asked what he thought of the experience of filming *The Cotton Club,* he replied, "I loved it." Pamela Koslow remembered things differently, however. "It was the worst. The tension was real thick most of the time." Problems were particularly evident during filming of the breakup scene. Hines recalled that "things were still tense from when I left. . . . That was very painful for Maurice—he wasn't ready to break up the act."

Playing the scene was painful for both brothers. In one day, they had to replay their splitting up at least eight times. Coppola was expert at getting them to relive the experience. "For a while, we were yelling at each other," Hines said. "And Francis just said, 'Oh, good, thank you.'" When the scene was finally finished, Gregory and Maurice were crying, as were their parents, who were visiting the set that day.

The real-life conflict between Gregory and Maurice was not the only piece of behind-the-scenes drama. Another was how Gregory got the part to begin with. The film's producer and original director, Robert Evans (he turned to Francis Ford Coppola to direct the film when production complications began to mount), originally wanted Hines for the smaller part of Cab Calloway and offered Richard Pryor, who was a much bigger star at the time, the role of Sandman Williams. Hines insisted on seeing the script before signing up for anything, but Evans was keeping that a secret. According to Hines, he sneaked a draft of the script out of Evans's office and read it. He definitely did not want the supporting role of Calloway; he wanted the main part—Sandman Williams.

When Hines confronted Evans, the two had a monumental argument, and Evans flatly refused to consider Hines for the part. At that point, Hines related, "I instituted a reign of terror on Robert Evans. I called him every day. I went over to his house twice again, uninvited. It got to the point where he was actually yelling at me over the phone, 'Stop calling me! I know you want the part.'"

Hines admitted he was extremely aggressive, although he denied that he crossed over the line into obnoxiousness. "Well, I got close on that one," he acknowledged. In the end, he got the role he wanted, playing the character of Sandman Williams.

Other production difficulties with *The Cotton Club* included a script that was still unfinished when shooting began. When a final script did finally appear, the actors were dissatisfied with it, so director Coppola kept working. He handed out fresh pages nearly every day of shooting, in what one actor called "a most unorthodox film experience."

Such a filming experience might put off many actors, but Hines felt it gave him a lot of creative room in which to maneuver. Richard Gere was the film's main star, and it was his name that had attracted much of the financing; therefore, his role was primary. Hines, however, continuously worked with Coppola to help create a black story line that would make the film's black characters as real and vibrant as Gere's.

Hines's costar, Lonette McKee, whose character had only five lines of dialogue in the script's early draft, remembered that Hines told her, "Don't get put off by the cheesy part. We're gonna be right up there with Richard and Diane [Lane], but what we've got to do is help Francis [Coppola] create." McKee laughed, "He was probably just saying that for moral support, but I'll tell you, [the black story line] was not there when we walked in."

When the project started, Hines appreciated the fact that the film could help present a positive image for young African Americans. He had a personal interest in the film as well, since his grandmother Ora had been a showgirl at the real Cotton Club. Hines also had fond memories of playing in a

Cotton Club revue in Miami when he was only 11. He had appeared then with Cab Calloway, who told the young tapper about the real Cotton Club and its famous entertainers. Undoubtedly the legend of the real Cotton Club contributed to Hines's eagerness to play a prominent part in the film and make it a movie that, he said, "Black people could be proud of—something that would show them as special."

Although the film was widely anticipated, the movie failed with both audiences and critics. The *New York Times* said that film was "not a complete disaster, but it's not a whole lot of fun . . . there is an air about it of expensive desperation." Gregory Hines himself received excellent reviews for both his acting and dancing, which said that "the best things in the film are its musical numbers [including] a terrific 'Crazy Rhythm' tap number danced by Gregory Hines and his brother Maurice, and an impromptu tap demonstration by Gregory Hines." Despite the film's failure, Hines's reputation emerged intact.

In 1985, Hines again displayed his formidable dancing skills in the critically acclaimed film *White Nights*, a thriller set in the former Soviet Union. (The title refers to the long daylight periods that occur during the summer in northern Russia.) Hines played Raymond Greenwood, an American dancer who defects to the Soviet Union to protest the racism of the draft during the Vietnam War. Hines starred opposite the legendary ballet dancer Mikhail Baryshnikov who, playing the character of Kolya Rodchenko, relived part of his own real life as a defector to the United States. Director Taylor Hackford freely admitted blending fact and fiction by drawing on the two artists' personal experiences in creating their characters.

In a plot filled with twists and turns, Kolya, who had defected, returns to the Soviet Union. He is nabbed by the secret police and forced to stay with Greenwood and his wife (played by Isabella Rossellini) in a sumptuous apartment in

In 1985, Hines partnered with Mikhail Baryshnikov, a world-famous ballet dancer, for the movie *White Nights*. In addition to showcasing their dance abilities, *White Nights* established Hines's and Baryshnikov's reputations as solid dramatic actors. They appear dancing together in a scene from the film, above.

Leningrad (now called St. Petersburg). Greenwood's task is to try to persuade Kolya to remain in the Soviet Union. As the plot develops, Greenwood (now wanting to return to the United States) and Kolya attempt to escape, giving the actors plenty of action and lively "thriller" scenes.

The plot, however, is merely a device to display the incredible dancing of Hines and Baryshnikov. Nine dance numbers enrich the film, including an intense and stirring solo by Baryshnikov, which expresses his anger and frustration at his nation's dreary oppression. In another scene, Hines, as Greenwood, half speaks and half taps the story of his struggle as a young dancer and his disillusionment with the American establishment.

What surprised critics were the dramatic talents of the film's stars. Baryshnikov was still best known as the world's greatest ballet dancer. Although Hines was well known for his dancing roles, his film credits had not yet established him as a leading dramatic actor. Both succeeded in bringing what one writer called "genuine emotion" to their parts. Hines was impressed with his costar. "He was acting while he was dancing," he exclaimed. "I thought, 'That is what I want to do. I want to speak of anger, frustration, insecurity, jealousy in my dancing.'"

Hines's character also challenged the popular view of black tap dancers as "novelty acts," versus the view of ballet dancers as artists. Hackford explained the film's concept: "What I was trying to do was get at the root of what the frustration of their lives as artists has been. . . . I think it's a real feeling that Greg had, and he was able to express it."

For the 1986 film *Running Scared,* Hines did not have to challenge anyone's view of dance. In fact, he did not dance at all in the film. He played a Chicago undercover cop who, with his partner (costar Billy Crystal), wanted to retire. For both Hines and Crystal, these were their first roles as leading men. The film was not a dramatic epic; rather, it gave Hines a crack at comedy and what one writer called "a finger-snapping style . . . that makes the whole thing click."

Both actors had to work out vigorously to build up muscle. Crystal remarked with his usual wit, "Once we read the script and knew we had to take our shirts off on page 62, we started to pump. Gregory is built like a greyhound, and when he started, he was very skinny." Hines was in the habit of channeling his assertiveness in whatever direction it needed to go. According to Crystal, "he attacks things. The day after we began working out, he had a body-building book and magazines like *You and Your Tendons* and *The Wonderful World of*

Thighs." If there was any question of Hines's talent or ability as a leading man, director Peter Hyams laid it to rest: "In terms of talent, Gregory is an absolute thermonuclear weapon just waiting to go off."

A major challenge that Hines found in his pursuit of a film career was the stereotypical views of tap dancing and tap dancers. Since the 1930s and 1940s, when the Hollywood musical was at its peak of popularity and Fred Astaire and his elegant costars (including Ginger Rogers) distracted Americans from the Great Depression with formal top hats and tails and fabulous evening gowns, few films have portrayed tap dancing. For Hines, who wanted a film career but saw himself primarily as a tap dancer, combining the two art forms of dance and film as well as overcoming racial prejudice was a huge job, but he overcame the obstacles and became a success.

In 1989, Hines got the chance to star in a film that showcased both his dancing and acting talents by presenting the personal story of a tap dancer named Max Washington. The movie, *Tap*, also told the story of what happened to some legendary tappers who continued dancing even after tap dancing was out of style. These dancers played themselves. Among the greats who appeared were "Sandman" Sims, Jimmy Slyde, Bunny Briggs, Arthur Duncan, Harold Nicholas, Steve Condos, and Pat Rico. Hines was especially drawn to the film because, as he said, "The charm of this movie is that these are the real people who lived the parts they are playing. Everyone connected with this film has their whole lifetime in it."

DID YOU KNOW?

Did you know that Gregory Hines was the first choice to play the Eddie Murphy role in the smash hit movie *48 Hrs.*? He was forced to drop out of the production, however, because of scheduling conflicts with *The Cotton Club*.

Hines played Max Washington, a tap dancer and the son of a great tap dancer who turns to the more lucrative business of crime when dancing as a career dries up. Returning from prison, Max is discouraged and saddened because he has abandoned his life as a dancer and believes there is no place for him to go. With the urging and encouragement of his girlfriend, Amy, and her father, Little Mo, played by one of Hines's idols, Sammy Davis Jr., Max reenters the world of tap dancing. He salvages his career when he and Little Mo create an entirely new style of dancing.

The film's director, Nick Castle Jr., is the son of Nick Castle, noted tap dancer and choreographer, who worked with film's tap greats in the 1930s and 1940s. Choreographer Henry LeTang also worked on the film. In addition to the cast of dance legends, the movie featured members of the new generation of dancers, including a young Chance Taylor and a very young Savion Glover, the tap sensation who would appear in *Jelly's Last Jam* and later receive raves for his own show, *Bring in 'Da Noise, Bring in 'Da Funk*.

Far from being nostalgic, *Tap* explored the reasons for the decline of tap dancing and its revival as a dance form. Indeed, half of the film is devoted to bringing tap into a modern, urban setting. The film was not a huge commercial success. It did, however, bring to the big screen the story of tap dancing in the last half of the twentieth century and showcased three generations of tap dancers in a lively story line that engaged its audience.

Gregory Hines's personality was a great asset in advancing his career in films. His director on *Running Scared* characterized him as a person with an "enormous wellspring of warmth. He's a real hugger, a kisser. I wanted that affectionate quality for the character." Costar Billy Crystal also praised Hines's personal character: "Gregory is the kindest person I've ever seen with people. He's totally unselfish." So whatever Hines's aggressiveness accomplished in driving his career forward, he balanced it with an affable personality that has undoubtedly made him many friends in the film industry.

Although Hines' film career was in full swing and had brought him his greatest fame, his heart belonged to Broadway. His next role, that of Jelly Roll Morton in the new musical *Jelly's Last Jam*, would be his biggest acting challenge yet and would provide him his greatest accolades.

8

The Role of a Lifetime

It was Sunday, May 31, 1992, and a star-studded audience waited expectantly as film and stage star Sigourney Weaver opened the envelope. Its contents would reveal the winner of the 1992 Tony Award for Best Actor in a Musical. "And the Tony goes to Gregory Hines!"

After more than four decades in show business, the lean and lithe tap dancer, actor, and singer had finally received the coveted award. Hines had been nominated three times before, but the honor had always gone to others. He remembered how he had felt when another person's name had been called: "It was such a harsh sound and the rush of emotion was such that it actually hurt." This time it was his turn, and it was different. "When I heard my own name, I got this warm rush that went through my whole body," he recalled.

Hines's mesmerizing performance as Ferdinand "Jelly Roll" Morton in the hit musical *Jelly's Last Jam* finally netted him the Tony. Not only was the role a career-defining break-through for Hines, but the production itself was a landmark in African-American musical theater. Until then, black musicals (with a few exceptions, such as *Dreamgirls*) had been revues that celebrated specific music or composers rather than people or characters. The *New York Times* called *Jelly's Last Jam*, which was honored with 11 Tony nominations, "the breakthrough musical of our time." The show explored the conflicts and inner lives of black Americans by portraying the life, character, and music of Jelly Roll Morton, a jazz pianist, a composer, and the self-proclaimed inventor of jazz. The role was the first to allow Hines to integrate all his talents in one performance and to give him the opportunity to explore the very same racial conflicts that had always been a part of his life.

The real-life Morton was born Ferdinand Joseph LaMothe in New Orleans in 1890 into a Creole family. By one definition, Creoles were descendants of African slaves and their white French masters. In early New Orleans, Creoles had all the rights and privileges of whites. By the time Morton was born, however, segregation and racial laws in Louisiana (the so-called Jim Crow laws) had deprived Creoles of most of their status as whites and placed them in the same category as blacks. Many Creoles, however, clung tightly to their French heritage, rejecting the culture and traditions of their black ancestors. Morton was born into this atmosphere of racial and class tensions.

A light-skinned Creole, Morton, like many others, denied his blackness and emphasized his white ancestry. Yet he found himself drawn to the vibrant music and rhythms of his African-American ancestors, and New Orleans at that time was the place to hear it at its best. From the black musicians of the city he heard blues and ragtime and the syncopated marching music of New Orleans black brass bands. He absorbed the sounds of the "rag man," the "gator man," and the "gumbo lady"

Jelly Roll Morton, the self-proclaimed "originator of jazz," is shown in 1938 in Washington, D.C., recording a documentary for the Library of Congress. Morton's tumultuous life was the basis for the Broadway show *Jelly's Last Jam*, in which Gregory Hines originated the starring role. In 1992, Hines won the Tony for Best Actor in a Musical for his role in the show.

as they cried their wares in the city streets. He frequented the notorious district of saloons and brothels known as Storyville, mingling with gamblers, dealers, pool sharks, prostitutes, and hustlers. When Morton was about 15, his great-grandmother threw him out of her house because of his association with what his family called the "lower orders" and people of darker skin. This set him out on his musical journey as a pianist, composer, arranger, band leader, and recording artist.

Morton was a controversial figure. Boasting of his French ancestry, he consistently denied his African-American roots and exaggerated his Creole background. He once told an interviewer, "All my folks came directly from the shores of France." He also claimed that the original spelling of his name was "La Menthe" because it sounded more French than "LaMothe." Yet at the same time, he continually sought out the company of disreputable people and began his career by performing in the saloons and brothels of Storyville. He drew much of his music from African-American roots.

Perhaps his greatest boast was that he himself had invented jazz, and he made this claim all his life. Although jazz was born in New Orleans, many musicians and composers were involved in its birth, and many jazz historians do not agree that Morton invented jazz. What he did do, however, was to brilliantly combine the blues and ragtime and New Orleans marching music—all the sounds of his youth—with the more formal music of his French heritage, creating his own innovative form of jazz. He is considered by many to be the most important of the New Orleans jazz composers and arrangers and, as Morton himself put it, "The world's greatest hot tune writer."

To produce a play about this contradictory and not always sympathetic figure was a challenge to the producers of *Jelly's Last Jam* and to its star, Gregory Hines. Indeed, when he first read the script, Hines rejected the role because he did not like the character he would have to play. He finally relented when his wife, Pamela Koslow, the play's coproducer, persuaded him to attend a workshop performance and meet with writer-director George Wolfe. Wolfe, who has become known since as a leading theater and television director, was then relatively unknown, but even still, Hines was impressed with Wolfe's talent. He also knew Wolfe was taking a risk in presenting a new kind of black musical.

Jelly was not to be the stereotypical black musical. As Hines said, "For too long on the musical stage we have perpetuated the myth that African-Americans are always singing and dancing and happy." Instead, through the contradictory, conflicted character of Morton, the play explores an extremely sensitive issue in black America—internal racial conflict. Hines later reflected on the play and his role in it.

> I loved being in shows like *Eubie!* and *Sophisticated Ladies,* but I knew they weren't really saying anything. *Jelly* is. One of the best kept secrets in the world is the racism that exists within the African-American community. And I knew that to have a piece on Broadway about the attitudes we have about hair quality and skin color and class would not only affect white and African-American audiences, but it would speak on larger issues of the human condition.

Hines also recalled that in his own family light skin versus dark skin was an issue: "My mother came from a very light skinned background. My father is dark-skinned, and when they fell in love her father refused to come to the wedding." For Hines, performing in the musical was not just an opportunity to use his talents as an actor and dancer in a major production. It gave him the chance to speak to the issue of racial conflicts within the African-American community.

Jelly's Last Jam is a journey through Morton's life. As the play opens, Morton is near death when a sinister figure called the Chimney Man appears and beckons him with the words, "Welcome, Jelly, to the other side. Time to tell your tale 'n' save your soul." As the play moves back through Jelly's life, the Chimney Man hovers nearby, constantly reminding Jelly of how he has denied his blackness.

Despite his commitment to the role, Hines had difficult moments during the rehearsal process. He thought about his own family as he worked on expressing Morton's racial atti-

Above, Hines (center, in striped coat) dances with other members of the cast of *Jelly's Last Jam*. Morton was a controversial figure in many ways, but Hines found his racial attitudes particularly hard to work with—Morton was light-skinned and denied his African-American roots.

tudes. During rehearsals, Hines had trouble saying such lines as "I [Morton] was classically trained while those of a darker hue lived in shacks and crooned the blues." Still, Hines overcame his anxieties, and sometimes even anger, as he delved into the role. He explained, "After I really got inside Jelly, I enjoyed saying his lines."

Some who followed Morton's life and career disagreed with the very concept of the play and the way Jelly's character was portrayed. Bob Greene, an expert on Morton's life and music, created and toured with his own show, *The World of Jelly Roll Morton*. Greene publicly criticized *Jelly's Last Jam*, insisting that "Jelly was not racist. He was a New Orleans Creole and all his recordings were with Black musicians. His idol was the pianist Tony Jackson, fully Black. . . . In contradiction to the very premise of the play, he knew his roots and drew his music from them." Hines and director Wolfe disagreed. "I think the play follows the truth very closely," Hines explained. "In fact, I think there have been areas of Jelly's actual life that have been softened to make him as palatable as he can be and yet still tell the story of his life."

Whatever the realities of Jelly's life, Hines faced difficulties other than the script. He had to do eight shows a week, and he was not in top physical condition. To prepare for the grueling role, he redesigned his diet and began lifting weights to get in shape. Another challenge facing Hines and director Wolfe was the fact that Morton was a pianist, not a tap dancer. Hines had to portray Morton's character through tap dancing, as well as acting and singing, rather than through playing the piano. Wolfe decided that none of the tap dances would be just for fun. Each would be designed to express different emotions and concepts. It worked. For two hours and 25 minutes every night, Hines tapped across the stage in his own distinctive style, shoulders a little still, legs moving in his distinctive graceful motions. Critic John Simon of *New York* magazine called Hines "the consummate leading man. Acting, dancing, singing, or just standing in emotion-filled stillness, he puts into this Jelly Roll a part of himself that is deeper than the part."

Playing Jelly Roll Morton is considered by many to be the crowning moment of Hines's long career, which was already full of impressive achievements. The challenge of playing Jelly Roll Morton forced Hines to go beyond anything he had done before in terms of creating and becoming a character. For Hines, *Jelly's Last Jam* was a personal triumph. Little did he know that it would be the last Broadway play in which he would appear.

A Legacy of Greatness

Professional entertainers are wise to ensure their futures. Careers come and go, and great parts in Broadway musicals are few and far between. So to keep busy (and in front of the public eye), diversifying their sources of income becomes essential. Gregory Hines, with his multitude of talents, had little to worry about in that regard. The recording industry, for example, was another way for him to use his talents. As early as 1987, he recorded a single with Luther Vandross called "There's Nothing Better Than Love." The song immediately went to Number 1 on *Billboard*'s black singles chart. A year later, he became a recording artist with Epic Records and launched his debut album, *Gregory Hines.* He sang eight songs, including "Love Don't Love You Anymore," "This Is What I Believe," and "I'm Gonna Get to You." The album was just a modest success, reaching Number 53 on *Billboard*'s top R&B/hip-hop albums.

In 2001, Gregory Hines starred in *Bojangles*, a made-for-TV movie chronicling the life of Bill "Bojangles" Robinson. Bojangles was a pioneering tap dancer in the late nineteenth and early twentieth centuries. He had great success with a solo act at a time when African-American artists were usually compelled to perform with at least one partner.

Gregory Hines achieved much greater success in other arenas of the entertainment world. Throughout the 1980s and 1990s and even into the last decade of his life, while appearing in films and on Broadway, he kept up a hectic schedule of television appearances and special shows. He made many television movies, including *Louisiana Black*, *T Bone 'N Weasel*, *A Stranger in Town*, and *The Cherokee Kid*. In a role dear to his heart, Hines starred in the television movie *Bojangles*, playing the role of the renowned tap dancer Bill "Bojangles" Robinson.

Hines also took part in a large number of television specials: participating in a birthday tribute to South Africa's president

Bill "Bojangles" Robinson

It was fitting that Gregory Hines should play the role of Bill Robinson in the TV movie *Bojangles*. In the movie, the greatest tap dancer of his generation plays homage to the greatest dancer of his era.

Bill "Bojangles" Robinson (May 25, 1878–November 25, 1949) was a pioneer and preeminent African American tap dance performer. He began dancing at the age of six just to earn a living, appearing as a "hoofer" or song-and-dance man, in local beer gardens. At the age of seven, Bill dropped out of school to pursue dancing.

Until 1930, Robinson performed in nightclubs and in musical revues. He was known for his dancing ability (including his famous "stair dance," during which he tap danced up and down a long flight of stairs), his gambling exploits, his bow ties of multiple colors, and his ability to run backward (he set a world's record of 8.2 seconds for the 75-yard backward dash). At his peak as a nightclub performer, he earned $3,500 a week, an enormous sum in those days.

With the decline of black musical revues, Robinson found work in Hollywood, appearing as a tap-dancing butler with Shirley Temple in five films. Audiences enjoyed his style, which was always cool and reserved; he rarely used his upper body, depending instead on his busy, inventive feet and his expressive face.

When he died in 1949, his body lay in state in Harlem; schools were closed, and thousands lined the streets waiting for a glimpse of the funeral procession. Politicians, both black and white, eulogized him perhaps more lavishly than any other African American of his time. Dance writers Marshall and Jean Stearns observed that "to his own people, Robinson became a modern John Henry, who instead of driving steel, laid down iron taps."

Nelson Mandela, sharing in a celebration of the performing arts from the Kennedy Center in Washington, D.C., hosting the Sixteenth Annual Black Filmmakers Hall of Fame, and performing in the PBS special *Gregory Hines: Tap Dance in America*, for which he won an Emmy Award.

Hines also appeared on *Saturday Night Live* (*SNL*) with legendary pianist Eubie Blake in what was one of the most acclaimed *SNL* episodes. It took some doing to get on the popular show, but Hines displayed the same boldness and assertive attitude he had shown in getting his role in *The Cotton Club*. He went to an *SNL* producer's office and claimed he had an appointment, which was not true. He waited for a time and finally left when he realized the producer was just letting him sit and wait. Back the next day, he told the same story to a secretary, insisting he had an appointment. When she told him that he was indeed in the appointment book, Hines was somewhat taken aback. "What? I am?" he exclaimed. He quickly recovered, however. "Obviously he'd told her if I came back he'd see me," Hines said.

Hines also made his debut as a director in 1994 with the film *Bleeding Hearts*. Shot in New York City, the movie is about the relationship between a black high-school girl and her 30-year-old white lover. Hines said he was intrigued by the idea of the culture and age difference between the black young woman and the older white man.

In 1997, Hines finally participated in a project he had held close to his heart for years. *The Gregory Hines Show*, a television comedy series, premiered on September 15, 1997. Certainly the show helped eliminate the dearth of prime-time African American-oriented shows airing on major television networks. It also contributed its own intelligence to the family-comedy scene.

Reviewers were enthusiastic about the show. Hines played Ben Stevenson, a single father in his 40s. Brandon Hammond was Stevenson's 12-year-old son, and Bill Cobbs costarred as Stevenson's father. One reviewer wrote that "the chemistry between Hammond and Hines is amazing, and their affectionate relationship feels real, and is quite touching. Hines is one of the most charismatic actors working today, and I'm glad to see him in something that does his talent justice." Unfortunately for Hines and his fans, the show was canceled in the spring of 1998, after airing only 16 episodes.

Just two years after the demise of his own series, Hines appeared in a television show that reached the largest audience of his career, guest starring on the smash hit television comedy *Will and Grace* during the 1999–2000 seasons. In the series, he played the role of Ben Doucette, a successful attorney with an on-again-off-again relationship with Grace Adler (Debra Messing), one of the series' title characters. In a couple of episodes, he even had a chance to show off his tapping skills.

Gregory Hines was a man whose talents were exceptionally elastic. Tap dancer, actor, singer, and drummer—was there anything he couldn't do? The bigger question is: Which talent was closest to his heart? According to Hines, the stage was his first love. "My roots in show business come from the live stage and that's where I belong," he declared. "My style is part choreography, part improvisation. That gives me a chance to show people the possibilities of tap dancing, which, at its heart, is mathematics with endless possibilities."

During the last years of his life, Hines lived in New York City's Greenwich Village, where he had shared a duplex with Pamela Koslow and their son, Zachary. His daughter from his first marriage, Daria, was married. Hines's apartment came equipped with a hot tub, an entertainment center, and a darkroom where he developed his own film. Despite the childhood injury to his eye, Hines was an avid photographer, working almost exclusively in black and white portraits. Despite his talent as a photographer, he worked only with people he knew and was comfortable with.

Hines also lifted weights to keep in shape and enjoyed watching football games. As a boy he was a pretty good football player. "I wanted to play football," he once said. "I wanted to follow that dream. Sometimes when I watch football games, I sit and dream to myself, 'Gee, if I had played football.'. . . That's the one thing I think about when I think of an alternative [career]."

Sometimes Hines enjoyed just breaking out into tapping to express his energy and exuberance. He really liked to tap privately in elevators. He told an interviewer: "For some reason, if I can get into an elevator and there's nobody else with me, there's a nice little boom and slap sound. . . . I've been able to come up with some really good steps in elevators, and later on I try to remember them."

What did Gregory Hines want to be remembered for? Despite being a genuine superstar, he did not have a problem explaining that family was really what mattered. "Oh, that's easy. I would like to be remembered with love by my family and friends, the people who really know me. When it all comes down to it, that's what's important in life. I never think in terms of anyone else remembering me—that would just be icing on the cake."

Gregory Hines realized that, as important to him as his talents were, they would not last forever, and no one, no matter how talented, could afford to neglect the most important parts of life.

Despite his devotion to his family, Hines and Pamela Koslow divorced in 2000. He remained close to his children, though. At the time of his death in 2003, he was engaged to bodybuilder Negrita Jayde. When reflecting on his life in 1992, Hines said,

> Sometimes when I think about the whole scheme of things, I think that being a parent is really why I'm here. Not to tap dance or entertain, but to love my children and teach them how to love so that they can love their children and the cycle is unbroken. That's why I get chills just thinking about a

grandchild—that I would be able to hold a child that comes from my child and know that my child can love this baby because I was able to love her because my parents love me. That's what it's all about.

LEGACY

During his phenomenal career, Gregory Hines performed as dancer, actor, and singer. Yet despite performing in a variety of mediums, he remained essentially a tap dancer. "It's the way I communicate best," he said. Where did he think tap dancing as a medium of expression was headed? In the late 1980s, he promoted his ideas about tap, explaining that the conventional image of a tap dancer as a slight person decked out in tails or tuxedo had to be shaken up. He pointed out that people are attracted to ballet and modern dance because they see beautiful, expressive bodies that are not swathed in clothing. Certainly Hines was instrumental in changing this image of the tap dancer and modernizing it to appeal to new, young audiences.

Hines fervently believed that tap dancing, long considered a form of entertainment but not a form of art, must "defend its choreographic integrity . . . particularly on the Broadway scene." He noted that, in the 1980s, most Broadway chorus tap dancing was created by choreographers who knew little about tap. They put together some basic steps, he explained, and tossed in some ballet. It pleased audiences, but it was not dazzling tap dancing.

There can be no doubt that by the 1990s the situation was definitely changing for the better, in no small part due to the influence of Gregory Hines. He felt very strongly that a solid base of talent was ready and waiting to take tap to new heights. He strongly urged using that talent, using the best tap dancers available, instead of encouraging mediocre performances by people who weren't primarily tap dancers. He described his ideas: "Our creative abilities can take wing because we have the people who can do the stuff. When we saw that group, that ensemble, tap dancing in the amazing way that we have seen in great ballet and great modern dance—it would have an impact." These dancers are, in effect, the children and students of Gregory Hines.

When asked about his young friend and protégé Savion Glover, whom Hines referred to with affection as "The Man," Hines conceded that Savion and other young dancers today were more technically skilled at tap than he ever was. Savion is tap's "wonder boy," Hines said, and described the young dancer's style:

> You know, I've tried many times to steal some of Jimmy Slyde's stuff and I can't get it. . . . But Savion can do Jimmy Slyde. He can do Buster Brown. He can do me and anything that Henry LeTang gives him. What's going to happen in five years, when this kid evolves into Savion? He'll have a sense of us inside him—and he'll be doing what nobody is doing. He is where tap dance is going.

Over the course of his still blossoming career, Savion Glover has had a phenomenal influence on the continuing development and popularity of tap. At the tender age of 11, Glover starred in the Tony Award-winning and hit Broadway show *The Tap Dance Kid*. He appeared in the 1989 film *Tap* with Hines and Sammy Davis Jr. and again with Gregory Hines in *Jelly's Last Jam*. Glover has also appeared on *Sesame Street*, where he can still be seen in reruns, and at the 1996 Academy Awards, where he danced a tribute to the late Gene Kelly.

This extraordinarily talented young man also choreographed and starred in the hit Broadway show and tap phenomenon *Bring in 'Da Noise, Bring in 'Da Funk*, which earned no less than nine Tony nominations, winning for Glover the Tony Award for choreography, as well as the 1996 Drama

Savion Glover, modern tap extraordinaire, was a protégé of Hines's; the two danced together in the film *Tap* and in *Jelly's Last Jam*. After Hines's death, Glover paid tribute to his mentor by displaying a portrait of Hines along with a pair of tap shoes. Glover also dedicated the number "Stars and Stripes Forever (For Now)," from his show *Classical Savion*, to Hines.

Desk Award, the Outer Critics Circle Award, two Obie (Off-Broadway Theater Awards) Awards, and two Fred Astaire Awards. The show highlighted the history of African-American dance in a Broadway musical style. Glover also won the 1991 Martin Luther King Jr. Outstanding Youth Award and was the youngest recipient to date of the 1996 Dance Magazine Award.

He expanded the possibilities of tap with his production *Classical Savion*. In it, he tapped to classical pieces played by a chamber string group and added drums and piano for a jazzier sound at the end of the concert. If anyone can build on the legacy of Gregory Hines and bring tap into the new millennium, it is Savion Glover.

In addition to *Noise/Funk*, several other shows have rocked the dance world by incorporating new elements into the traditional artistry of syncopated dance. *Tap Dogs*, created by Australian steelworkers; *Stomp*, performed by a troupe of English stage actors; and Michael Flatley's lightning-speed Irish dancing in *Riverdance* and *Lord of the Dance* have all spread the popularity of the dance form to almost unprecedented levels. "We did a study and were just overwhelmed by the diversity of the audience . . . it's the full range of people from 5 to 95," Michael Flatley noted.

These new dance shows that have swept the performance world have several aspects in common, including elements that Gregory Hines predicted would help modernize tap and spread it to new audiences. The beauty of the dancers' bodies is one factor. "These acts exude a different kind of sexiness from ballet or other forms of dance," said one reviewer, "the kind you get when a rock singer takes off his shirt." How much further from a stereotypical tapper in a white tie and tails can you get?

These shows also include a rock-and-roll spirit, which appeals to younger audiences. *Lord of the Dance* in particular uses light shows and other elements of rock concerts to wow its audiences. Music critics have noted that tap can easily incorporate hip-hop and rap, encouraging young dancers to tap dance to contemporary music.

The new styles also display an athletic spirit and heat that has often been missing from dance in the past. Previously, the goal of many kinds of performance dance had been to mask the difficulty, to make the dancing appear effortless. Today's style is to let the audience see the athleticism and effort it takes to perform new dance styles, lending the entire performance a raw power and energy unimaginable 30 years ago. All of these shows seem inconceivable without the example and influence of Gregory Hines.

The percussive sounds of tap, particularly in the show *Stomp*, also take on a new style. The group uses trash cans, sticks, car keys, and brooms, among other objects, to create an irresistible rhythm—with practically no accompanying music. *Tap Dogs*, an Australian tap show, uses only the sound of steel-workers' boots hitting the stage floor.

One last element completes the picture. It is what theater critic Lawson Taitte called "working-class chic." These performers—Michael Flatley, Savion Glover, and Sheldon and Dein Perry of *Tap Dogs*—make no secret of their working-class origins and, in some cases, capitalize on it. In *Tap Dogs*, the cast wears jeans and steelworkers' boots and welds the set together. The performers in *Stomp* are depicted as janitors. With their aura of ordinariness, combined with brilliant talent, the appeal of these shows is nearly irresistible to the average man, woman, or kid. Just as Hines predicted, audiences are dazzled.

It is sad that Hines was not alive to participate in the resurgent popularity of tap dancing, in all its glorious new forms. Everything that the new generation does, every innovation that it makes, continues his legacy of innovation in tap, keeping his memory alive.

Even if he had survived, he, like all dancers, would have aged. Hines was always painfully aware that the day would have come when he wouldn't be able to dance professionally: "Skill diminishes with age; it's just mathematics," he conceded. He referred to a fellow performer when he said, "Like Nipsey Russell said, 'I'm not as good as I once was, but I'm as good once as I ever was.'" He went on,

> There are steps I could do in film all day that I couldn't do eight shows a week. Gene Kelly and Fred Astaire would do steps for 40 seconds or a minute and a half on film, and then "Cut! Break!" That's how they stayed so young. Jimmy Slyde is dancing and he's in his mid-fifties, and Bunny Briggs,

who's in his early sixties. They can still do sixteenth notes!
I want to carry on their legacy—so that one day it will be
Jelly's Last Jam with Savion Glover, featuring Gregory Hines
as the Chimney Man. I'm going to tap-dance until I can't!

Watching Gregory Hines symbolically pass the torch on to
Savion Glover onstage in *Jelly's Last Jam* would have been a
magical theatrical moment. In a sense, it has happened already.
Just as Hines picked up and expanded the legacy of dancers
like Fred Astaire, Jimmy Slyde, and the Nicholas Brothers,
Glover and hundreds of other dancers have picked up and
expanded on Hines's legacy and made it their own. In this way,
he has achieved immortality as a dancer.

Appendix

SELECTED ACCOMPLISHMENTS

FILMS

1981 *History of the World, Part I; Wolfen*

1983 *Deal of the Century*

1984 *The Cotton Club*

1985 *White Nights*

1986 *Running Scared*

1988 *Off Limits*

1989 *Tap*

1991 *Eve of Destruction; A Rage in Harlem*

1992 *T Bone N Weasel* (TV movie)

1994 *Renaissance Man; Bleeding Hearts* (directed)

1995 *Waiting to Exhale*

1996 *The Cherokee Kid* (TV movie); *Good Luck; The Preacher's Wife*

1999 *The Tic Code*

2000 *Things You Can Tell Just by Looking At Her; Once in the Life*

2001 *Bojangles* (TV movie) (actor and producer)

2002 *The Red Sneakers* (TV movie) (actor and director)

MUSICALS AND STAGE PERFORMANCES

1978 *Eubie!; The Last Minstrel Show*

1979 *Comin' Uptown*

1980 *Black Broadway*

1981 *Sophisticated Ladies*

1985 *Night of 100 Stars II*

1988 *An Evening of Tap*

1989 *Twelfth Night*

1992 *Jelly's Last Jam*

TELEVISION SHOWS AND APPEARANCES

1954 *The Ed Sullivan Show*

1963 *The Tonight Show Starring Johnny Carson*

1985 *About Tap; The American Film Institute Salute to Gene Kelly; Motown Returns to the Apollo*

1986 *An All-Star Celebration Honoring Martin Luther King, Jr.; The 40th Annual Tony Awards*

1987 *The 19th Annual NAACP Image Awards*

1988 *Freedomfest: Nelson Mandela's 70th Birthday Celebration; The 42nd Annual Tony Awards*

1989 *Gregory Hines: Tap in America* (also called *Dance in America*); *The 61st Annual Academy Awards Presentation; The 21st Annual NAACP Image Awards; The 16th Annual Black Filmmakers Hall of Fame* (syndicator, host)

1990 *The Stellar Gospel Music Awards* (syndicator); *Sammy Davis Jr.'s 60th Anniversary Celebration*

1991 *The Kennedy Center Honors: A Celebration of the Performing Arts; The Dancing Man—Peg Leg Bates*

1992 *Jammin': Jelly Roll Morton on Broadway* (also choreographer)

1994 *Baseball* (miniseries, voice)

1997 *Subway Stories: Tales from the Underground*

1997-1998 *The Gregory Hines Show*

1999-2000 *Will and Grace*

1999 *AFI's 100 Years . . . 100 Stars*

2000 *The Kennedy Center Honors; It's Black Entertainment*

2002 *The Tony Awards*

1946   Gregory Hines is born to Alma and Maurice Hines on February 14 in New York City.

1949   He begins learning tap steps from brother, Maurice Jr.

1952   Gregory begins performing professionally with brother as the Hines Kids.

1954   Hines Kids perform at Harlem's Apollo Theater.

1962   Hines Kids tour nightclub circuit in United States; appear on television (*The Ed Sullivan Show, The Jackie Gleason Show*); perform in Europe.

1963   Maurice Sr. joins the act, and the name is changed to Hines, Hines and Dad; tour United States and Europe; appear on *The Tonight Show Starring Johnny Carson*.

1968   Hines marries Patricia Panella; settles in New York City.

1971   Hines's daughter, Daria, is born.

1973   Gregory leaves Hines, Hines and Dad; moves to Venice, California.

1974–1977   He leads hippie lifestyle; founds jazz-rock band; writes unsuccessful songs; works as busboy and teaches karate; is divorced from Patricia Panella; meets future wife Pamela Koslow.

1978   Hines returns to New York City; lands role on Broadway in *The Last Minstrel Show*; appears in show *Eubie!* and is nominated for a Tony Award.

1979   He appears in musical *Comin' Uptown* and is nominated for second Tony Award.

1981   He marries Pamela Koslow; stars in *Sophisticated Ladies* and is nominated for third Tony Award; makes film debut in *Wolfen* with Albert Finney.

1982   Hines tours United States with *Sophisticated Ladies*.

1984   He stars in film *The Cotton Club* with brother Maurice Jr.

1985 He films *White Nights* with Mikhail Baryshnikov; appears in PBS special *About Tap*; begins touring as a soloist.

1986 Hines films *Running Scared* with Billy Crystal.

1987 He records first single "There's Nothing Better Than Love," which hits Number 1 on black singles chart; performs onstage in Jazz Tap Ensemble.

1988 He performs *An Evening of Tap* onstage; records album *Gregory Hines*; films *Off Limits* with Willem Dafoe.

1989 Hines plays Feste the Clown in *Twelfth Night*; stars in film *Tap*; appears in PBS special *Gregory Hines: Tap in America*, which wins Emmy Award.

1991 He films *Eve of Destruction* and *A Rage in Harlem*.

1992 He stars in *Jelly's Last Jam*; wins Tony Award for Best Performance by a Leading Actor in a Musical; appears in PBS special *Jammin': Jelly Roll Morton on Broadway*.

1994 Hines directs film *Bleeding Hearts*.

1995 He stars in television movie *A Stranger in Town*; films *Waiting to Exhale*.

1996 He films *Good Luck, Mad Dog Time*, and *The Preacher's Wife*.

1998 Hines produces and stars in television series *The Gregory Hines Show*; canceled in 1998; films *The Tic Code*.

1999 He films *Once in the Life*, appears on television series *Will and Grace*.

2000 Hines stars in theatrical film *Once in the Life* and television movie *Who Killed Atlanta's Children*; divorces second wife Pamela Koslow.

2001 He plays Bill "Bojangles" Robinson in television movie *Bojangles*.

2002 He cohosts *The Tony Awards*.

2003 Gregory Hines dies of liver cancer on August 9.

Frank, Rusty E. *TAP! The Greatest Tap Dance Stars and Their Stories 1900–1955.* New York: Da Capo Press, 1995.

Glover, Savion. *Savion!: My Life in Tap.* New York: HarperCollins, 2000.

Guerrero, Ed. *Framing Blackness: The African American Image in Film.* Philadelphia: Temple University Press, 1993.

Hill, Constance Valis. *Brotherhood in Rhythm: The Jazz Tap Dancing of the Nicholas Brothers.* New York: Cooper Square Press, 2002.

Kantor, Michael, and Laurence Maslon. *Broadway: The American Musical.* New York: Bulfinch, 2004.

Lomax, Alan. *Mister Jelly Roll: The Fortunes of Jelly Roll Morton, New Orleans Creole and "Inventor of Jazz."* Berkeley: University of California Press, 2001.

Null, Gary. *Black Hollywood: The Black Performer in Motion Pictures.* New York: Citadel Press, 1975.

Rees, Heather. *Tap Dancing: Rhythm in Their Feet.* Wiltshire, UK: Crowood Press, 2003.

Rhines, Jesse Algeron. *Black Film/White Money.* New Brunswick, N.J.: Rutgers University Press, 1996.

WEB SITES
TheatreDance.com
www.theatredance.com/mainstage.html

Tapdance.info
www.tapdance.info

United Taps: Moving at the Speed of Sound
www.unitedtaps.com

Picture Credits

PAGE

Index

About the Author

Dennis Abrams is the author of numerous books for Chelsea House, including biographies of Anthony Horowitz, Hamid Karzai, Ty Cobb, Eminem, Beastie Boys, George Washington Carver, Xerxes, and Jay-Z. He attended Antioch College where he majored in English and Communications. Dennis currently lives in Houston, Texas, with his partner of 19 years and their two dogs and three cats.